Jean-Luc Aubarbier
Michel Binet

Wonderful Périgord

Photographs by Nicolas Fédiaevsky

Translated by Angela Moyon

EDITIONS OUEST-FRANCE
13 rue du Breil, Rennes

The forest around Brantôme.

The village of Beynac.

*The Romanesque abbey church
in Saint-Avit-Sénieur.*

*Front cover :
Laussel Castle in Marquay.*

*Back cover :
A fortress-cave in La Madeleine.*

The old bridge in Saint-Jean-de-Côle.

INTRODUCTION

Périgord's geography and economy

Although for administrative purposes, it is part of the Aquitaine Region and forms its northern border, the County of Dordogne (the third-largest in France with an area of 9,225 sq. kms.) lies within boundaries that are almost exactly the same as the frontiers of the old province of Périgord. It lies between the cristalline slopes of the last outcrops of the Massif Central to the north-east and the rich alluvial plains of the Aquitaine Basin in the south-west, and its main rivers are the Dordogne, Isle, Dronne, and Vézère. Its geographical position provides such a wide variety of landscapes, vegetation, and climatic conditions, that it is more correct to speak of Périgord in the plural. Traditionally, a distinc-

tion was drawn between Central Périgord (around Périgueux), Green Périgord (north, north-east, Nontron, Jumilhac), Dark Périgord (south-east, Sarlat), the Bergerac Area (south, south-west) and White Périgord or the Ribérac Area (north-west). In addition to these five subdivisions, there are areas of thick forest such as Double or Le Landais (west), and the rocky outcrops of the Quercy Plateau around Nadaillac, Daglan, and Thenon. In this mosaic of a landscape with a plethora of highly-characteristic charms, its population of some 380,000 (as compared with more than 500,000 in the last century) is spread unevenly through the county but still has a very marked rural profile. Apart from a number of large industrial sectors such as wood and timber products, leather, shoes, and food-

processing, most of the county's activities are farm-based (cereal crops, stock-breeding). Périgord is the top French producer of tobacco and strawberries, and is the second largest producer of walnuts and fattened poultry. This, then, is Périgord.

Underground Périgord - prehistoric Périgord

Périgord has numerous prehistoric caves that are open to the public and all of them are worth a visit. There are caves full of rock formations, of course, like the ones in Domme or Le Grand Roc in Les Eyzies. There are swallowholes like the one in Proumeyssac near Le Bugue. But, most of all, there are the most famous prehistoric caves known to man at the present time (48

3

of them in all). It is here, in the most privileged area anywhere in the world, that prehistoric remains are to be seen at their densest. There are hundreds of sites, rock shelters, and caves where our far-distant ancestors living tens of thousands of years before the pyramids were built left voluntary or involuntary but very moving traces of their time here on earth. And what traces ! When faced with the painted splendours of the ceilings in Lascaux, "Prehistory's Pope", Father Breuil, described them in the only way possible, "This is Prehistory's Sixtine Chapel." The original cave is closed to the public because the huge number of visitors would have impaired this unique heritage for all time, but a few yards away is a fac-simile, an admirably faithful, precise and realistic reproduction of the cave that enables visitors to admire the famous friezes.

Although Périgord cannot claim to be the cradle of humanity (even if Cro-Magnon Man was discovered there), it was in its valleys and along its yellow ochre cliffs overlooking the rivers, that man created Art. Many of the sites in Dark Périgord have given their names to cultural industries that are representative of certain periods, e.g. Mousterian and Magdalanian, to name but the best-known. As a natural consequence, it was here too that the science of prehistory was born and has developed since the end of last century. The greatest prehistorians (Capitan, Peyrony, Leroi-Gourhan and Breuil) all worked here. In addition to Lascaux, Breuil catalogued two other caves in Les Eyzies that are considered as being among the six most beautiful anywhere in the world - Font de Gaume and Combarelles, even though the charm of their engravings and paintings of horses, ibex, reindeer and bison is somewhat more hesitant. Further on, in Rouffignac, visitors journey into the entrails of the earth on a train that takes them through the miles of galleries in the Cave of the One Hundred Mammoth. This, in short, is the exceptional prehistoric wealth of the "Land of Mankind", of the world's capital of prehistory, Les Eyzies, and of the royal road that has been listed as part of mankind's heritage, the Vézère Valley.

Historic Périgord

Little is known of our ancestors, the Petrocorii. They joined with other tribes in rebellion against Rome, but their resistance ended in tragedy in Uxellodunum, the land of our neighbours and friends in Quercy. Much more spectacular because they are concentrated in two or three main sites, are the remains from the Gallo-Roman Period - a gigantic half-ruined tower and an arena in Périgueux (originally known as Vesuna), wonderful collections gathered from numerous archaeological digs and now displayed in the Périgord Museum, the large-scale remains of a villa in Montcare, and a Roman tower in La Rigale Castle in Villetoureix. The first man-made grottos, some of them underground

Le Thot : a reconstitution of a prehistoric dwelling.

*The Roc de Cazelle near Les Eyzies :
these holes once contained the rafters of the cave dwellings.*

and others high up on cliff faces, probably date from this period. Some of the underground shelters and aerial watchtowers could accommodate entire populations. Julius Caesar states that the Gauls were already taking refuge in them at that time, and it is a known fact that this type of shelter was used throughout the troubled times of the Middle Ages. They are to be found throughout the county, and there are very few cliffs that do not contain at least one.

After the barbarian invasions and a brief period of occupation by the Visigoths in the 5th century, Périgord was annexed to Clovis' kingdom as a result of the Battle of Vouillé. It then suffered the vicissitudes of his successors' policies. The almost general state of confusion reached its height during Pippin the Short's repeated campaigns against Duke Waffre of Aquitaine. In the end, the Duke was assassinated, probably in the Double Forest. The region gained county status under Charlemagne (and a number of religious establishments benefitted from his generosity when he travelled through the area), before being subjected to ransack and pillaging by the Vikings for more than a century from 850 A.D. onwards. For a short time, Périgord became part of the Angoulême region, during the reign of Charles the Bald, before passing to the House of La Marche from which the Talleyrands were descended, shortly before the year one thousand A.D. The family provided Périgord with several Counts and governed the region for five hundred years. Day-to-day life in the locality gradually became more organised, despite famine, outbreaks of plague, and the constant threat of armed gangs who still thought of themselves as "barbarians from the north". The oldest aristocratic families came into existence at this point - the Taillefers, Birons, Hauteforts etc. Their independent spirit was summed up perfectly by Count Adalbert of Périgord. When Hugh Capet asked him, "Who made you a Count?", he retorted, "And who made you a King?"

It was in the 11th and 12th centuries, a period during which the feudal system slowly took shape, that the first architectural masterpieces were created. All over the region, hundreds of Romanesque churches came to life, most of them very humble constructions but some of them typically Périgordian with magnificent domes over hanging keystones (St. Front in Périgueux, Cherval, Trémolat, etc.). The Ribérac area has some especially outstanding examples. This was truly a period of

Commarque.

awakening, transformation, and development. The art of the troubadours blossomed with Arnaud Daniel, Arnaud de Mareuil and, more particularly, Bertrand de Born. Romanesque carvings and frescoes decorated the churches, like invitations to prayer (Besse, Cénac, Grand-Brassac, etc.). Abbeys and priories belonging to the Benedictine, Cistercian and Dominican Orders, Knights Templars' commanderies and preceptories, all show the strength of the Christian faith. This

was a period of renewal; they were also times of uncertainty. Since Guyenne had been annexed to the Plantagenet Crown (after Eleanor of Aquitaine's second marriage in 1152), Périgord automatically passed under English sovereignty. In fact, situated as it was on the edges of the spheres of influence of both crowns, it was to swing from one dynasty to the other over many years. It was ripped apart by more than three hundred years of almost continuous fighting until the end of the One Hundred Years' War in 1453, but the constant battles also shaped its landscape.

Just as they had done previously during the Viking invasions, the local people sought refuge in the man-made caves and the numerous fortress-caves. The most famous sites (La Roque-Saint-Christophe and La Madeleine) were also inhabited way back in prehistoric times. The parapeted towers, bartizans and crenelations of splendid, austere, fortified churches such as Saint-Amand-de-Coly, Tayac, Trémolat, and Paunat jutted up above the stone-slabbed roofs of the houses nestling in the protective shade of their massive walls, as if seeking warmth. The whole area bristled with proud,

redoubtable fortresses. Beynac, Castelnaud and Commarque are prestigious examples, to name but a few. From the 13th century onwards a number of towns developed to the west and south, deliberate creations and mostly the result of orders from the King or the Count. These were the fortified villages, or "bastides". They attracted a stable population, were granted English or French charters, and were built to a geometric layout around a central arcaded square. Domme, Monpazier and Beaumont have maintained their mediaeval charm to the full.

As the One Hundred Years' War had finished in 1453, the late 15th and early 16th centuries saw the development of urban architecture in the Castillon Plain and along the banks of the R. Dordogne. Périgueux, Bergerac and Sarlat adorned themselves with their finest Gothic and Renaissance mansions. In rural districts, the nobility commissioned most of Périgord's 1,200 castles, manorhouses and small country residences.Catching a glimpse of them at the head of a valley, round the bend of a road, or at the top of a rise, is sure to delight even the most difficult seeker of beauty. Many of the buildings are markedly warlike in character and in the second half of the 16th century, they were attacked, pillaged, and subjected to fire, for the Wars of Religion reached an unusually violent stage in Périgord. At that time, Bergerac was, with La Rochelle, one of the mightiest Protestant strongholds in France. After the wars, Périgord, which belonged to Henri of Navarre, was annexed to the Crown once and for all and thereafter suffered the ups and down of French political life, from the Revolution until the tragic days of the Resistance Movement. Traces of its history, both ancient and modern, are to be found in its castles. They also keep alive the memory of the region's most famous literary figures - Bertran de Born, Michel de Montaigne, Etienne de la Boëtie, Brantôme, Fénelon, Maine de Biron, Eugène Le Roy, and André Maurois. Or its great leaders - Talleyrand, Saint-Exupéry, Biron... and even Joséphine Baker. Some of the ruins (La Chapelle-Faucher, l'Herm, etc.) hold memories of the tragedies that occurred there. Several of the castles are open to the public and some of them, like Bourdeilles or Mareuil, house quite remarkable collections.

In addition to its castles, churches, fortified villages and fortress-caves, Périgord still has some delightful villages from days gone by, with covered market, dovecots, stone huts or "bories", church, abbey and castle(s). Among them are Saint-Léon-sur-Vézère, Condat, Saint-Jean-de-Côle, and La Roque-Gageac, all of them veritable architectural gems. As for the old districts in Périgueux or Bergerac, now renovated and laid out as pedestrian precincts, they have regained all the charm of bygone days. Some small towns, such as Brantôme, Issigeac, Eymet or Mareuil, have resisted the occasionally over-obtrusive transformations of modern living. And Sarlat and Dark Périgord are worth a special mention.

A goose farm.

Gastronomic Périgord

There are certain words that conjure up pleasures of a more Rabelaisian nature than castles, landscapes, churches or caves. They are delightful terms that tickle the palate of gourmet and gourmand alike. What are they? Preserved goose ("confit"), pâté with truffles, duck breasts, flap mushroom òmelette, stuffed neck of goose, walnut cake etc. Enough to damn the souls of the strictest supporters of low-calorie diets. Let us be honest - Périgord's cooking finds it difficult to cater for that sort of nutrition. The food is rich, nourishing, and based mainly on healthy farm produce. It is rustic, tasty country fare, which prestigious chefs have adapted to suit modern eating habits. Here in Périgord, it is not uncommon to see somebody at the next table pour wine into his plate after finishing his soup or "tourin" and lap it up - this is called "faire chabrol". Food here is based on a long tradition of rural eating habits.

In such a short introduction, it is impossible to mention all the characteristic features of Périgord food but it would be a grave error, if not a sin, not to take advantage of a stay in Périgord to try all the very varied local produce. Taste the "mique" (pork with dumplings) that Jacquou le Croquant so enjoyed on Christmas evening. Try the "pastis", the apple cake that our neighbours in Quercy also make so well. And you must try the preserved goose, duck, Sarlat-style potatoes, Périgueux sauce, partridge with morels etc. There are the wines from the Bergerac region to try too - Monbazillac, Pécharmant, the Montravel that Montaigne so appreciated, the Saussignac praised by Rabelais, and then... then, there are the truffles, the rare, highly sought after black diamonds that...but let us stop there and leave gourmets the unutterable pleasure of discovering for themselves the finest gems of a culinary art that, for many of our compatriots, is a veritable way of life, a "science of eating".

Périgord now and forever

With such a rich artistic heritage (both prehistoric and historical), is is hardly surprising that a very special type of tourism that could be described as "cultural" has sprung up in this region, for it is true that people do not come to Périgord by chance. But even if caves and castles had no more secrets to share with visitors, people would still have thousands of new things to try - a trip downstream in a canoe, forest walks, solitary hamlets in places where the road suddenly runs into a farmyard or duckpond. They would still have the Gallic hillforts to see, "Caesar's encampments", the numerous paths taken at will. Visitors can stay in any of the many hotels, campsites, bed and breakfasts, and farm-inns which have been providing high-quality accommodation for the past twenty years. Moreover, the farm-inns enable visitors to live in the country and to learn about the one thing that is Périgord's true wealth -its people.

This is what we should like to invite visitors to share. If their travelling habits are like those of Montaigne, and they never draw "any known line, no straight lines, no curves", if in fact like the most famous of all Périgord's sons, they take time to look properly and not just see, to feel and to taste, then and only then Périgord, like a beautiful woman, will reveal all its charms. That's the truly Wonderful Périgord.

An old street in Bergerac.▶

Dark Périgord
SARLAT

Sarlat, the geographical centre of the Périgord-Quercy region is by far and away the **most popular place with tourists** anywhere in the region. Almost one million visitors come to see this mediaeval gem every year - some for the first time, others to rediscover it. With its population of 10,000, this sub-prefecture in the County of Dordogne is now top of the list of tourist and cultural centres. Although it is mainly a shopping and business community, it does have some industries, in particular a large factory making surgical probes and several food-processing companies, some of them specialising in **foie gras.** And it is the foie gras, considered to be among the very best in France, that has helped to give Périgord in general and the town in particular their reputation as a culinary paradise. Dark Périgord, of which Sarlat is the capital, owes its name to the dark foliage on the green oaks and the rest of its vegetation. And it has truly magical scenery to offer visitors. The **"golden triangle"** between the Vézère Valley (the centre of world prehistory) and the Dordogne Valley with its Flamboyant Gothic castles has managed

to retain its secretive yet welcoming appearance.

Although Sarlat is one of the largest **mediaeval towns** (13th-16th century) in the world, it cannot boast a very long history. The first abbey was probably founded between 820 and 840 A.D. by Duke Pippin of Aquitaine. **St. Bernard,** the incomparable saviour of souls and redoubtable orator, stopped in Sarlat in 1147 when on an evangelical mission to the south of France. Black Death was rife there at that time. He gave blessed bread to the sick and brought about their cure. This event, one might almost say this miracle, was commemmorated by the building of the strange "Lantern of the Deceased" which is still one of the town's emblems. The town, which had expanded in the shade of the religious community, gradually obtai-

The countryside round Sarlat : the Enéa Valley.

ned its independence. Taxes were abolished in 1204, and **consuls were elected** from 1223 onwards. The 4 consuls and 24 aldermen were the forerunners of our town councils. They administered the town's affairs and had legal powers. In 1317, Pope John XXII, who was a native of the

11

Sarlat : stone-slabbed roofs.

Quercy region, created the **Bishopric of Sarlat,** thereby separating it from the Périgueux diocese. During the One Hundred Years' War, Sarlat was never invaded by the English in spite of the Black Death that wrought havoc in the ranks of the defending forces. The traitor Donadei, who hatched a plot to hand the town over, was **sewn into a sack and thrown into the Cuze.** The Treaty of Brétigny (1360) left the town in English hands and the famous Captain, John Chandos, received its keys. But when fighting broke out again in 1370, Sarlat rallied to the fleur-de-lys banner of Charles V, encouraged by Du Guesclin who had come to rekindle the warring ardour of the burghers. From 1404 until the final victory, Sarlat's troops played an active part in the retaking of Périgord and victory cost them dear - the

diocese lay in ruins. Between 1450 and 1500, half the houses in the town were rebuilt in a style that was already **Renaissance** (most of the town's architectural masterpieces date from this period).

Armand de Gontaut Biron, who was named Bishop of Sarlat in 1492, undertook to complete St. Mary's Church on which building work had been started in 1368. In 1533, another bishop who was related to Catherine of Medici, one **Nicolo Gaddi** of Florence, had the Italianate bishop's palace built next to the cathedral. Despite a renewed outbreak of plague in 1521-1522 which caused 3,000 deaths, the mid 16th century saw the development of thriving cultural activity in Sarlat. Renaissance humanism did not prevent an explosion of religious fanaticism. In 1562, Duras besieged the town - it was liberated by a royal army. In 1574, for the first time in its history, Sarlat was taken by storm

under the leadership of **Geoffroy de Vivans** who scattered St. Sacerdos' relics before being chased out in his turn.

Lost in the depths of distant Périgord, Sarlat could have fallen into oblivion had it not been for the **Malraux Law** passed on 4th August 1962 that benefitted only four towns in France. Perhaps the Minister of Culture remembered his days in the French Resistance in the heart of the Sarlat forests when he signed the **Renovation and Restoration Act.** The work undertaken from 1964 onwards under the guidance of the Director of the Historic Monuments Dept. (the French ''National Trust''), Y.M.Froidevaux, and the architects M.Robert and P.Prunet, brought to the attention of the public a veritable treasure trove of **mediaeval and Renaissance architecture.** Tourists and film directors then took it upon themselves to tell the whole world about Sarlat, a corner of the

Sarlat : the enigmatic Lantern of the Deceased.

globe "that is the nearest thing to heaven" as Henry Miller himself put it.

But let us now turn to the most famous of Sarlat's sons - **Etienne de La Boétie** (1530-1563). It is high time he was introduced, not merely as a friend of Montaigne's, but more especially as one of his century's great thinkers with ideas that are still relevant today. Opposite the cathedral is the splendid house where he was born on **1st November 1530,** into a respectable bourgeois family of tradesmen and magistrates who had

Sarlat : rue de la Liberté.

Sarlat : the Vassal Mansion.

provided several of Sarlat's consuls since the 13th century. He was a brilliant student at Orléans University and was very receptive to new ideas (his teacher, Anne du Bourg, was burnt at the stake on the place de Grève in Paris for heresy). He was at home among the intellectuals of Sarlat and Orléans where he used to meet Dorat and Baïf. It was at this time that he wrote his **Discourse on Voluntary Servitude.** It was an inflammatory text, likely to take him to the stake, and it was passed secretly from hand to hand. It was not published (by the Protestants) until after his death. La Boétie is also the author of many **poems,** one of which was a famous sonnet dedicated to the R. Dordogne. At the age of 23, he entered the Bordeaux Assizes as an Assessor and married a young widow named Marguerite de Carle. In 1558, he met **Montaigne,** who was three years younger than

him and was already one of his admirers ("we had been seeking each other before we had ever set eyes on each other"). Montaigne always considered him as his philosophical mentor ("He surpassed me by an infinite distance"). Their exemplary **friendship** lasted for five years and can be summed up in the famous sentence taken from the Essays, "If I am asked why I loved him, I know that the only way to express it is to say that it was because he was him and I was me". In June 1563, Sarlat was again hit by plague. La Boétie fell ill in Germinan, at Montaigne's brother-in-law's house. He died on 18th August 1563, attended by his friend to whom he left his library and his precious manuscripts.

Let's start our visit of the mediaeval town by the **Place de la Grande Rigaudie.** In the centre, the petrified stone figure of Etienne de La Boétie passively observes the flow of visi-

tors. The Rue de Tourny (once the main street) leads to the **Place du Peyrou** on which stands St. Sacerdos' Cathedral. Just before reaching the square, you will see on your left, at the corner of Rue Bonnel, a fine 17th-century mansion and, on the right, the **Bishop's Palace** with its double-mullioned windows, built by Bishop Nicolo Gaddi. An elegant Italianate gallery was added to this rather austere building decorated with atalantes, human faces, and heads of monsters, in the 20th century. There are three listed buildings opposite the entrance to the church. The one with the timbering dates from the 16th century, and another one, formerly an inn, from the 18th. The third building, which stands out from the rest and is one of the town's emblems, is the superb **La Boétie Mansion.** The highly-ornate façade is a masterpiece of **Renaissance** architecture and shows the Italian influence. It has **carved mullioned windows** framed by medallions and pilasters. At the top are decorated dormer windows and tall chimneys. Outside, note the stone roofing slabs, the gable ends carved with crockets, and the **sheep** on the walls - they were the La Boétie family emblem.

St. Sacerdos' Cathedral was once a Benedictine minster before becoming the see in 1317. Of the Romanesque building that replaced a Carolingian construction, all that remains is a **porch-belltower.** Its doorway was recarved in the 17th century. It is topped by **five statues** of unknown origin (one of them is said to represent Atlas carrying the world). They are very difficult to date. Of the three storeys in the 18th-century onion tower, the lower one has tall blind arcading and the other two have bay windows. The church

remained in its unfinished state from 1318 to 1790. Most of the building is 16th century - the great nave with its four spans, and the two side aisles with their ribbed arching supported by massive pillars. At the end is a five-sided chevet with an ambulatory running round it, and an older chevet. The **rich furnishings** include a number of carved reredos, a pulpit decorated with a tetramorphe and 18th-century choirstalls. There is also an 18th-century loft containing a genuine **Cliquot organ,** one of the finest in France, with a pair of bellows that make the old walls vibrate during concerts. The ogival-vaulted sacristy is the former 14th-century chapter house. Leave the church by the south aisle and walk round the building. You will find the tiny **Blue Penitents' Chapel** (also known as St. Benedict's). The interior is built in a

pure Romanesque style. Now let's cross the Cour des Fontaines and the Cour des Chanoines surrounded by fine houses. A semi-circular opening hidden in one corner of the wall leads to the **Penitents' Garden** (or garden of tombstones). The town's former graveyard is overlooked on one side by the huge mass of the cathedral and, on the other, by the strange cutline of the **Lantern of the Deceased.** It is a peaceful, charming spot used for entertainment during the summer months (concerts, plays). On the other side of the apse are the **tombs,** stone niches which once contained the stone coffins of Sarlat's VIP's. A flight of steps leads up past **a fine wayside cross** to the Lantern of the Deceased. Nobody knows what this strange 12th-century construction in the shape of a mortar shell or rocket was really used for.

Sarlat : a close-up of the cathedral doorway.

After crossing the hilly Rue Montaigne with its old houses, you will reach the narrow **Rue d'Albusse.** At nos. 2-4, a huge building with three main sections was once the scene of **General Fournier-Sarlovèze**'s escapades. At the end of the Rue d'Albusse, at 1 Rue de la Salamandre (the street that leads down into the heart of the town), stands the **Grézel Mansion.** Its polygonal tower contains a 15th-century doorway decorated with a salamander, a legendary animal featured on Sarlat's coat-of-arms. Above the Grézel Mansion, at 6 Rue du Présidial, is the **Genis (or Beaupuy)** Mansion, a 15th-century construction that underwent modification during the 18th century. It has a pilastered porch topped by a triangular pediment and a canopied gallery. On the right, in the Rue Landry, is one of the loveliest of all the town's buildings - the **Law Courts** that housed the **tribunal** established by Henri II in 1552 and which, in the 17th century, had up to ten public prosecutors and thirteen members of the bar. Its two huge windows with their loggia, and its wall covered with Virginia creeper below a strange **lantern turret,** have a charm all of their own. At the end of the Rue du Présidial flanked by a number of houses built directly into the town walls, is the Rue Fénelon.

On the left at no.16 is a 16th-century mansion. Beyond it is the **Salignac Residence,** dating from the 15th and 18th centuries, where Fénelon's aunts used to live. It is decorated with a gargoyle and, on the back, there is a Gothic window. Opposite, at no. 13, is the fine 16th-century Aillac Mansion which has a polygonal tower, Renaissance windows, and a pointed chimney. This building, which was also used as a convent by the Sisters of the Faith in the 17th century, is also known as the Mirepoiser Mansion. As you go down the street, take a look at nos. 8, 10, 12 and 14, four 15th-century houses with Renaissance windows. At no. 6, there is a 17th-century gate. At no. 3, at the end of a courtyard, is the **Gérard (or du Barry) Mansion**

Sarlat : the Court House.

17

Sarlat :
Etienne de la Boétie's birthplace.

dating from the 14th and 18th centuries. It is now in a very dilapidated condition but was once one of the finest houses in the town. The huge building still has a pillared gallery, a gateway with a pediment over the top, and a Gothic window. At No.1 Rue Fénelon, right at the end of the street, there is an attractive rounded building dating from the 17th century. The ground floor has open arcades and the dormer windows upstairs are all carved. In the inner courtyard is the tower of a 15th-century residence with a Gothic porch decorated with carvings of human characters.

The fine **Town Hall** erected in 1615 by Henri Bouyssou, an architect from Monpazier, stands on the Place de la Liberté in the centre of Sarlat. The ground floor has covered arcades and the upper floor has a balustered balcony topped by a frieze. A small bell turret rises from the roof. The magnificent **Place de la Liberté** (once the Place Royale) lined along the whole of one side by old houses to which arcading brings a lighter touch, is an orderly and pleasant corner of the town. It serves as a backcloth for the **Drama Festival** and has inspired nearly all the film directors who have ever come to Dark Périgord to shoot scenes - from Jacques Estaud for Sans Famille, to Frank Roddam for La Promise, via Robert Hossein who set up the gallows there for the Misérables. Opposite the town hall at nos. 5 and 6 is a 17-century arcaded house and next door, at no. 7, is the splendid **Vienne Mansion** (or Maleville Mansion) with its double façade. It was originally the home of Jean de Vienne, superintendant of finances under Henri IV, and later belonged to the descendents of the jurist, Jacques de Maleville. It is a veritable castle in miniature. Set slightly back is a square staircase tower and a **Renaissance doorway** with a tympanum decorated with medallions representing Henri IV and Gabrielle d'Estrées (or Mary of Medici). On each side of the house, which has a corbelled turret, there are mullioned windows. On the square, the Tourist

18

Information Office is housed in a former shop with three outstanding **Renaissance windows** on the upper storey. Inside is a French-style ceiling and a painted, carved fireplace showing a stag between two dogs. Below the mansion, an alley runs into a covered passageway. Opposite the Vienne Mansion, at no.5, is the 14th-century **Dautrerie Mansion.** There is an old shop on the ground floor and, at the top of the gable end, is a carving of a leopard. The entrance, which is hidden away in a cul-de-sac, opens onto a magnificent Renaissance staircase. Beyond the square, the **Rue de la Liberté** flanked by old houses looks down to the cathedral belltower. On the right is a **chemist's shop** with a round tower followed by three half-timbered houses (nos. 2, 4 and 8). In an alleyway is the carved Gothic gateway with a fine studded door belonging to the **La Mothe Residence.**

If you turn to the right behind the La Boétie Mansion, you will find yourself in a network of **small courtyards** separated by vaulted passageways, a perfect example of mediaeval town planning. It is a muddle of half-timbered houses, corbelling, and turrets. You get the impression that you are about to run into a cul-de-sac at any moment but the alley goes through a small doorway and continues out on the other side. Take the **Rue Albéric Cahuet** from which you can see old houses, the former hospital and the back of the Vienne Mansion. You will get to **St. Mary's Church,** built from 1368 to 1479, which you may have spotted from the place de la Liberté. The building was damaged and the now non-existent chevet has been replaced by a window. The nave still has two spans and is roofed with stone slabs. There are also side chapels, and a warlike tower which has lost its top, decorated with statues and monstrous **gargoyles.** Go round the right-hand side of the church and you will see the sumptuous 16th-century **Chassaing Residence** (also known as the Magnanat or Gisson Mansion). It consists of two buildings connected by a hexagonal staircase tower and it forms a splendid natural backcloth for the Drama Fes-

tival. One of the buildings has a triple Gothic window with colonettes and a mullioned Renaissance bay window, side by side. Beyond it, the **Rue Magnanat** runs up to the house of the **Notary Royal** with its wonderful 17th-century gateway, before continuing on downwards, with some more interesting porches on the way. On the other side of the church is the **Rue des Consuls,** once the main street and the site of all Sarlat's VIP houses. At no. 9 on the right-hand side, standing on the tiny goose market square, is the 15th-century **Vassal Residence,** arguably the most picturesque mansion in the town

Sarlat : the Vienne Mansion.

with its double bartizan connecting the two buildings set at right angles and its mullioned windows. At no. 14 stands the Labrousse Mansion dating from the 17th century. Further on, on the left-hand side at nos. 8-10, is the most famous mansion in Sarlat, the **Plamon Residence** built by the great consular family of drapers who were raised to the peerage in the 14th century. Nowadays, it houses the drama festival offices and art exhibitions. The centuries have added their own styles to the mansion's architecture yet it has remained a pleasantly well-ordered building. The ground floor and first storey have 14th-century ribbed arching, a veritable piece of lacework in stone, while the second storey has mullioned bay windows dating from the 15th century. The porch and staircase tower date from the 17th century. The façade has a number of **carvings** (some of them obscene, others of dogs and people) and the hooks that were used to hang out flags and tapestries on feast days. Immediately opposite are the cool waters of the ogival-vaulted **St. Mary's Fountain** and the 15th-century **Mirandol Mansion** whose porch is topped by a pediment. At the corner of the street set at right angles is a fine **stone squinch**, topped by a terrace and a wrought-iron grid. It was placed there to enable carriages to turn the corner. The **Tapinois de Betou Residence** at no.6 has a remarkable 17th-century wooden staircase. Beyond it is the Rue des Consuls which leads to the main street.

Before visiting the western end of the town, take a quick look at the main street, the Rue de la République or the **Traverse** as the locals call it. It was laid between 1837 and 1840 through the heart of the old urban districts.

Opposite the Rue des Consuls is the **Rue des Armes** which seems to be barred by a splendid **timbered house** with ribbed vaulting dating from the 15th century. At no.2, the 15th-century Ravilhon Residence has ogival and mullioned windows. A 15th-century house spans the street which runs in front of the 14th-century guardhouse and the moneylenders' house before climbing to the remainder of the North Gate (the Turenne Breach) and the ramparts. Take the rue de la Charité to the **Rue J-J. Rousseau.** This will take you past the **White Penitents' Chapel** with its huge 17th-century doorway including columns and a pediment. It now houses the **Museum of Sacred Art.** Originally, it was part of the **Recollect convent,** built between 1615 and 1628. Beyond the Monméja Mansion with its 17th-century façade, at no. 9, is the vast **St.**

Clare's Convent dating from the 17th century. It has a corbelled turret. It was used as a prison during the French Revolution then as a hospice after being skilfully restored by the Old Manor Club. It is now **open to the public.** Leave the picturesque **Toulouse Hill** on your left with its venerable houses built in steps and stairs. Turn left into the **Rue de la Boétie** and, at no. 9, you will find the **Maynard Residence,** a 15th-century building with ogival windows, mullioned bays, and a fine walnut staircase. The end of the street loses itself in a whole network of alleyways. Let's go up the narrow **Rue Rousset** where you can see the 15th-century **St. Clar Mansion** and its round tower with machicolations, the **watchtower.** The building is a miniature castle, with Renaissance bay windows and a corbelled turret. At the top of the hill, turn left into the **Rue du Siège** where there is a string of old houses - 15th-century at no.6, 14th-century with Gothic windows at no.8 and, at the corner of the Rue des Trois Conils, the 17th-century Cerval Mansion. The right-hand side of the road is close to the town walls (which can be seen from the Rue de Turenne). There is a gate in them and they are overlooked by the **Hangman's Tower.** Before reaching the Traverse, go up the Rue du Barry and take the **Rue des Trois Conils** on the right.

The old house with its 15th-century tower containing a spiral staircase is the **Marzac Residence.** It was here that Madeleine Marie de Bart died in 1791. She was the daughter of Jean Bart and the wife of the Lord of Veyrignac. The Rue des Trois Conils disappears beneath a covered passageway adorned with windows set at a slant and leads to the **Place Liarsou,** to a superb **timbered house with a balcony** where the Boyt de Mérignac family used to live. They were related to La Boétie. The **Rue de Cordil** on the left provides a view of the other side of the St. Clar Mansion with its Renaissance windows. The Rue de La Boétie on the right crosses the main street and brings you back to the cathedral.

Above the Place de la Grande Rigaudie are the **Plantier Gardens**

laid out by Le Nôtre at the request of Fénelon. They bring a little freshness to the town centre and provide an attractive panoramic view of the rooftops of Sarlat. To the north near the former hospital, a fine 18th-century building that has recently been restored, is the brand new **Arts Centre** which is used for drama, concerts, and exhibitions. Not far away in the Rue du Cdt Maratuel, the **Aquarium Museum** is also brand new. It has some one hundred fish on show (trout, pike, salmon, sturgeon etc.).

Sarlat is a place of intense cultural activity, especially in the summer

months. Most of the activity revolves around the **Drama Festival** created in 1962 under the aegis of J. Boisserie. This festival, which is the most important one of its kind in Aquitaine and the oldest in France after Avignon, is one of the country's 7 or 8 major festivals.

SALIGNAC
11 miles N-E of Sarlat

Salignac is a pleasant village where a stroll through the narrow streets brings visitors face to face with 13th- and 14th-century Périgord houses, an old covered market, and a 14th- and 15th-century Gothic church. Rather strangely situated below the village is the impressive **Salignac Castle,** which is **open to the public.** This is one of the region's oldest fortresses. In fact, it is known to have existed in the 11th century and was rebuilt in the 12th and 13th centuries. Much of the castle as we see it today was built in the 15th and 17th centuries. The old fortress, which belonged to the **Salignac de la Mothe-Fénelon** family, ancestors of the Bishop of Cambrai, played an important part in the One Hundred Years'

Salignac : the village and castle.

War and the Wars of Religion. In 1545, the castle passed to the Gontaut-Biron family who made the austere citadel into a Renaissance residence. The tall 15th-century central section, whose two storeys are surrounded by ramparts, is roofed with stone slabs and pierced with mullioned lights. Next to it are two round towers topped by pepper pots, and a rectangular keep with flat piers. Inside, in the armoury hall and great drawing room, are fine 15th- and 16th-century fireplaces.

The South of Dark Périgord : The Dordogne Valley
◄SAINTE MONDANE - FENELON
11 miles S-E of Sarlat

Lost in the mists of the early Middle Ages, the origins of the village of Ste Mondane are a blend of history and legend. In the 8th century, the governor of Aquitaine, Amicius, gave **Laban** and his wife, **Mondane,** responsibility for the administration of the Sarlat region. They founded Calviac Abbey and their son, **St. Sacerdos,** became Bishop of Limoges and patron saint of Sarlat.

Above the village, overlooking the R. Dordogne and the **Bouriane Woods,** is **Fénelon Castle** which is **open to the public.** It was built in the 15th century and is an attractive blend of mediaeval warlike fortress and Renaissance aesthetic country house. At the southern end is a Renaissance residence flanked by two circular towers and pierced with fine dormer windows that have carved pediments. At the eastern end is a square pavilion dating from the 15th century and two round towers from the 14th and 15th centuries, one of which contains the private chapel where Fénelon used to pray. The west wing is a blend of mediaeval and Renaissance architecture. It is connected to the main building by a round staircase tower. Not far away is a very deep well. On the north side is a 17th-century gallery and a terrace decorated with a balustrade. A double **staircase** and a drawbridge lead up to the main courtyard. Visitors see, among other things, the loft whose mighty chestnut rafters support the impressive mass of **stone slabs** (one metric tonne per sq. meter) that roof the building. They also visit François Salignac de la Mothe Fénelon's **bedroom.** He was born here on 6th August 1651.

In the 17th century, after the death of his first wife who had already given him eleven children, **Pons de Salignac** married **Louise de La Cropte-Chantérac,** the mother of the famous writer. After a childhood spent in the castle, he began a course of study in Cahors University in 1663 under the guidance of his uncle, the Bishop of Sarlat. He continued his studies in Paris until 1672, under the protection of another uncle, Marquis Antoine de Fénelon. He entered the seminary and was ordained a priest c. 1675. He abandoned his vocation as a missionary for health reasons, and was first of all sent to **Carennac** in the County of Lot where he was the local priest before becoming Head of the "New Catholic" Convent from 1678 to 1689. He made use of this experience to write his Treatise on the Education of Girls. He became tutor to the Duke of Burgundy, Louis XIV's grandson, in 1689. It was for his pupil that he wrote the *Fables,* the *Dialogues of the Dead* and *Telemachus,* his main work written between 1694 and 1696. He was elected to the French Academy on 7th March 1693 and appointed Archbishop of Cambrai on 4th February 1695. From 1697 to 1699, there were the famous verbal jousts between **Bossuet,** the "Eagle of Meaux" and Fénelon, the "Swan of Cambrai". Fénelon, who defended the Quietism so beloved of Madame Guyon, a mystical proceeding which Bossuet considered as a dangerous heresy, was defeated by his redoubtable rival, disgraced by the king, and exiled in 1699 to his Archbishopric of Cambrai where he died on 1st January 1715 at the age of 63. He had been a teacher, moralist, and political reformer but he had not succeeded in having his ideas accepted, and the premature death of the Crown Prince in 1710 put an end to his dreams of becoming a government minister. Although he was far from his native region, Fénelon adorned his writings with Périgord's landscapes and characters. Many a reader of Telemachus recognised Sarlat in his Salente, the ideal city of Mentor the Sage. He particularly criticised the absolute monarchy, condemning the ill-effects of war and promoting the idea of a return to rural morals and a healthy lifestyle. Living as he did at the beginning of a century that was to become known as the Age of Enlightenment, he can be considered as the **precursor** of Montesquieu, Voltaire, and Rousseau.

Montfort : part of the castle.

◀ *The Dordogne Valley :*
the Montfort Meander.

MONTFORT
5 miles S. of Sarlat

Although Montfort Castle cannot be seen from a boat on the river, it is visible from the Montfort "**Cingle**" coming from the Carsac direction, where a meander of the Dordogne (the "cingle") encloses the Turnac peninsula. In the distance are the white cliffs of Caudon. Montfort, which dominates the landscape as if suspended in mid-air, seems to have stepped out of a fairy story. Its cliff face is full of caves, as if it were trying to hurl the castle down into the waters below, like the town of Ys. The old houses in the tiny village nestle at the foot of their mighty guardian in an apparent effort to keep warm.

The **castle's** history is marked by its strong will to survive. What a strange, tumultuous destiny it had ! Besieged and demolished on many occasions (1214, 1309, 1350, 1481, and 1606) and just as often rebuilt, the castle we see today is the result of eight centuries of building work. At the beginning of the 13th century, it belonged to the cruel Cathar lord, **Bernard de Casnac** and his wife Alix de Turenne, who mutilated any Catholic who fell into their hands. Men had their feet and hands cut off and their eyes put out ; women had their breasts and thumbs cut off. In 1214, during the Albigensian Crusade, the terrible **Simon de Montfort** (it is pure chance that he had the same name as the castle) sent troops to capture the castle. Legend has it that Bernard's daughter, Blanche, was burnt alive and that her ghost still haunts the fortress.

DOMME

8 miles S. of Sarlat

Built on a plateau overlooking the Dordogne Valley, the **Domme acropolis,** a town built for warfare, is an aesthetic and architectural masterpiece. It stands in an exceptionally beautiful setting, and its old houses are all built in an extraordinarily uniform style, pale golden stone topped by brown tiles, and balconies full of flowers.

At the beginning of the 13th century, the present town did not yet exist as such but, in its place, was a **castle** called Domme-Vieille. In an attempt to contain the English advance, Philip III the Bold, who realised its strategic importance, purchased part of the plateau in 1280 and founded the **fortified village** of Mont-de-Domme. The town was built between 1280 and 1310, but not without difficulty. Access was problematical, the population was very poor, and the work force was paid in leather coins made in Domme itself, called obsidionals. Thereafter, the town maintained the privilege of minting its own money. Gradually, Domme was built, the finest fortified village in Périgord.

In 1346, the English took the town by treachery, after the inhabitants had opened the gates for them. In the following year, the Seneschal of Périgord liberated the town and had the traitors hung. In 1348, Philip VI de Valois granted it a charter guaranteeing its autonomy. The One Hundred Years' War saw Domme pass from one camp to another and back again. The English besieged it in 1369 and captured it in 1393. The French then besieged it in 1421.

After more than a century of peace, the Wars of Religion brought Domme back into the limelight again. In 1572, the Huguenot Captain, **Geoffroy de Vivans,** twice failed to capture Domme. Neither siege nor treachery opened the gates of the town for him. He was even wounded in the attempt. On 25th October 1588, an insanely brave exploit enabled him to succeed at last. Captains Bordes and Bramarigues, escorted by thirty men, climbed the Barre de Domme cliffs at night. They were left undefended because they were thought to be impregnable. Once in the citadel, they opened the gates and Vivans took the town. In 1741, Domme was the birthplace of the jurist, **Jacques de Maleville,** one of the authors of the Civil Code.

Let us begin our visit to Domme by walking round the ramparts. The early 14th-century wall with its redans covers several hundred yards. It has three gates - the Del Bos, which was once fortified with a portcullis, the La Combe which leads down to a fountain, and the remarkable **Tower Gate** (Porte des Tours), the finest fortified gateway in Périgord built in the late 13th century. It was originally protected by a drawbridge and a portcullis and is now

Domme : the Tower Gate.

Domme : the ramparts.
A stone bench and slit window.

which is the heart of the town, stands the **Governor's House** dating from the 15th and 16th centuries, flanked by a corbelled turret. The 17th-century covered market hides the entrance to the **Jubilee Cave,** full of rock formations, which is **open to the public.** It is 3/4 mile long and contains a fairytale world of white stalactites and stalagmites. The bison and mammoth bones that are on show were uncovered when the entrance corridor was built. The Paul Reclus **Museum** houses discoveries made in Domme and has a particularly large section on Prehistory. Another museum, dealing with traditional Périgord, has just been opened, in the Garrigou House.

Beyond the parish church with its 17th-century belltower-wall is the famous Domme Bar, the most famous **panoramic view** in the whole of Périgord, a sheer drop of almost 490 ft. down to the meanders of the Dordogne and its fertile plain used for agriculture.

If there are indeed places in the world that seem to increase the creative capacity of writers, then Domme is one of these "inspired hills". To Henry Miller who visited it before the war, it was the source of inspiration for the introduction to one of his best-known works, **The Colossus of Maroussi.** Listen to what he has to say about Périgord as seen from the top of the Domme Bar, and a fine plea it is for our country, "It is a land of enchantment jealously marked by poets and only they have the right to claim it as their own. The nearest thing to heaven...A heaven, in fact, whose existence must go back thousands and thousands of years. I am convinced that it was just that for Cro-Magnon Man. Nothing will prevent me from believing that, if Cro-Magnon Man settled here, it was because he was highly intelligent and because he had a well-developed sense of beauty...Nothing will prevent me from believing that this great pacific region of France is destined to remain for ever a sacred place for mankind and that, when the cities have finished exterminating poets, their successors will find refuge and a cradle here..."

defended by two enormous round half-towers with bossages. They were once used as guardrooms and, from 1307 to 1318, as a place of imprisonment for Périgord's Knights Templar, who covered its walls with inscriptions and drawings.

Begin your visit to the town with the Rue Eugène Le Roy containing the house where Périgord's own author lived. It leads to the Place de la Rode, or "Roue" (wheel), where public executions were held. It has four fine houses, including the one that once belonged to the minter of coinage. It has triple windows. The main street is flanked by noble-looking houses, with ribbed arching and old doorways. At the corner of the Rue Geoffroy de Vivans, there is a carved window dating from the Renaissance period. In the Rue des Consuls, the former town hall has a 13th-century façade topped by a tower. On the Place de la Halle,

Domme : the covered market.

Domme : the Dordogne Valley ▶
and the cliffs of La Roque-Gageac
seen from the "Domme Bar".

Domme : a shopping street.

La Roque-Gageac : the church.

La Roque-Gageac and its cliffs. ▶

LA ROQUE GAGEAC
8 miles S. of Sarlat

Ranked third in the list of French beauty spots, after Mont Saint-Michel and Rocamadour, La Roque Gageac was given the envied title of "the most beautiful village in France" a few years ago. Its castles and houses, that are unusually similar in colour and style, nestle at the foot of the steep **cliff** crowned by green oaks, huddled against the rock face as if they would like to merge with the majestic surroundings and be reflected in the green waters of the R. Dordogne. The brown-tiled houses seem to have been hewn out of the white mass of the tall cliff. Depending on the position of the sun and the time of day, all the possible shades of yellow ochre, white and grey transform the village and its watery reflection into a veritable fairytale of sparkling colours.

In fact, in the Middle Ages, it was a small but prosperous free town with a population of 1,500 governed by two consuls. The Bishops of Sarlat had their country house there. The harbour in La Roque Gageac had a thriving business in timber, wine, iron, salt and foodstuffs of all kinds.

You really have to stroll through the alleyways that seem to run across the rooftops if you want to appreciate all the charms of the village. There is an attractive 14th-century church with a belltower-wall. Its apse forms an extension to the rock on which it is built. There are also some charming Périgord houses surrounded by quite astonishing Mediterranean vegetation which grows here because of the micro-climate created by the sun as it heats the rock. As you climb, you will discover a very fine **panoramic view** of the valley.

Downstream, almost on a level with the road, is **La Malartrie Castle.** Although it is built in a Neo-Gothic style, it does not stand out from the mediaeval backdrop. One family from La Roque Gageac dominates local history - the **Tardes.** Their **manorhouse** has an elegant round tower roofed with slabs and is flanked by two buildings with gable ends pierced by mullioned windows. If you had taken a stroll near the castle c. 1615, whether you were upper class or a mere yokel, you might have seen a strange, elongated instrument pointing in the direction of Orion or Andromeda. You would not have known what this was but no doubt you would have bowed low to the famous canon bending over the ocular instrument. **Jean Tarde,** who was born and who died in La Roque Gageac (1561-1636) brought back from his second trip to Italy the very first astronomical telescope to be seen in Périgord, and one of the first in France. He had acquired it from his friend, **Galileo.** It has to be said that, in his day, Jean Tarde was as famous as his elder, Pic de la Mirandole, and, if history has forgotten Jean Tarde, it is because the humanist canon who was also an astronomer, numismat, geographer, theologian, philosopher, and historian, preferred the solitude of his manorhouse and the background of his Dark Périgord to the crowds and wood-panelling of princely palaces. This **universal genius,** who in many respects is reminiscent of Leonardo da Vinci, was also interested in mechanics, mathematics, and even medecine and archaeology (long before Champollion, he sited Uxellodonum at Capdenac). It is said that, during a trip to Rome in cognito, he submitted such a brilliant thesis that the astounded sovereign pontif exclaimed, "If you are not Tarde, then you're the Devil".

Beynac and its castle.

◄*La Roque-Gageac.*
On the left is La Malartrie Castle.

Fayrac Castle opposite Beynac,►
with Castelnaud in the background.

BEYNAC
6 miles S.W. of Sarlat

The **setting** of Beynac and its castle is without doubt one of the most beautiful in France. The village, which was originally a collection of cave-dwellings, was built up in terraces on the banks of the river, perpendicular to a 490 ft. **cliff** topped by an impressive **fortress**. This "eagle's eyrie would appear austere if it did not have the sun to dust the golden walls with light and the Dordogne to act as a mirror". The ever-changing colours, and the luminosity of the stone, sky and water make Beynac a paradise for painters and photographers at any time of the year.

After the County of Périgord came into being, the castle was the seat of one of the four Périgord baronies, along with Biron, Bourdeilles and Mareuil. The first unequivocal trace of a Lord of Beynac goes back to 1115. The castle was so mighty and its barons so cruel that local vassals and peasants nicknamed it "Satan's Ark".

In 1214, when Simon de Montfort was returning from the Albigensian Crusade, he captured Beynac whose master was a friend of Raymond of Toulouse, and razed its defences to the ground. The One Hundred Years' War found Beynac in the French camp. In 1360, the Treaty of Brétigny brought it under English control but eight years later the Beynacs took up the struggle again beside Charles V. The English were never able to capture the citadel. In 1370, the only heiress to the estate, a little girl of three, was betrothed to her uncle, Pons de Commarque. He chased the English out of the Sarlat region and became the most powerful lord in the whole of Périgord.

The castle had natural defences on the river side, because of the sheer cliff, but it strengthened its defences to the north. A double wall, two moats, two barbicans. It is from here that we shall begin our visit. Built, modified, and embellished from the 13th to the 18th centuries, it is described by Jean Secret as "a synthesis of the art of building and the art

of defending oneself throughout the centuries". On each side of the **mighty 13th-century keep** are the main buildings, one dating from the 13th century but altered in the 16th and 17th centuries, and the other (containing the apartments) dating from the 14th and 17th centuries. Inside, the Great Hall of State where Périgord's nobility used to meet has ribbed vaulting and a carved Renaissance fireplace. The walls in the **private chapel** are decorated with 14th-century frescoes. Painted in a naive style and, as was common in the Middle Ages, showing a mixture of characters from various periods, they illustrate the Last Supper where St. Martial is acting as Head Waiter, Christ at the foot of the Cross, and the lords of Beynac. The apartments are decorated with wood-panelling and 18th-century painted ceilings. Visitors enter the keep by a narrow staircase and a low door. From there, there is a striking panoramic view of the entire valley and its castles. The **castle chapel** on the edge of the cliff is roofed with stone slabs. It dates from the Romanesque period.

Castelnaud : the mediaeval fortress.

◄Beynac : One tower in the castle houses the Protohistory Museum.

CASTELNAUD
6 miles S.W. of Sarlat

Standing guard over the confluence of the Dordogne and Céou, in a natural passageway between Quercy and Périgord, is **Castelnaud Castle.** It is one of the most beautiful ruins in the region, and it seems to surge up above the mediaeval village that takes the hillside by storm. This reminder of troubled times in days gone by is **open to the public.** So, let us climb up through the village of old Périgord houses, some of them carved, all of them roofed with stone slabs, and we shall come face to face with the enormous pile of pale golden stones that was once the castle.

The base of the castle dates from the 12th century. As one of the sides was afforded natural protection by the sheer cliff overhanging the R. Dordogne, the north face was strengthened in the 14th and 15th centuries by casemates and bastions designed to protect the drawbridge. The path to the village was a weak point, so a curtain wall flanked by two towers was added in the 15th century. On the south-western side, two barbicans were built. To the south, the oldest section, dating from the 12th and 13th centuries, is set out in a triangle around a tall 12th-century **keep** flanked by a vast **round tower** with walls 13 feet thick built by the English in the 15th century. The dates speak for themselves. Castelnaud is the most authentic example possible of a mediaeval fortress.

It was during the One Hundred Years' War that rivalry broke out between Beynac and Castelnaud. Near neighbours, each as powerful as the other, they struggled to achieve mastery of the Dordogne Valley. It is, then, scarcely surprising to find them in opposing camps at the outbreak of the war. Standing as it did in the heart of the conflict in Aquitaine, Castelnaud changed hands on numerous occasions. The English took it five times. The French did not finally regain the fortress until ten years before the Battle of Castillon. At the end of the 15th century, **François de Caumont** and his wife, Claude de Cardaillac, left the austere stronghold and had Les Milandes Castle built. Castelnaud was no more than a garrison. The Caumonts were Huguenots and at the outbreak of the Wars of Religion, the castle was held by the famous captain, **Geoffroy de Vivans,** who was born in Castelnaud. It was

Castelnaud : fortifications in the castle.

Castelnaud : the church.

at this time that the true story of **Anne de Caumont** took place. Her mother, Marguerite de Lustrac, remarried and her second husband was the master of Castelnaud, **Geoffroy de Caumont,** a moderate Huguenot. They usually lived in Les Milandes, but after the St. Bartholomew's Day Massacre (1572), they thought it advisable to take refuge in the old fortress. It was but a short stay of execution for Geoffroy de Caumont who was murdered by his squire, Anet de Commarque, shortly after the birth of his daughter. Anne was then one of the richest heiresses in France. Henri III designated the child's uncle, Jean des Cars, a Catholic with a solid reputation, to take care of her estate. But Marguerite, who had never taken her husband's faith as her own, rejected the choice and shut herself up in Castelnaud under the protection of Geoffroy de Vivans, a staunch Huguenot but with an even greater sense of fidelity to the Caumonts. When Jean des Cars discovered that Marguerite was seeking a match with the Biron family for her daughter, he decided to marry Anne, who was then 8 years old, to his eldest son, Prince Claude de Carnecy, a boy of 13. He had the girl kidnapped and quickly had the marriage solemnized. Five years later, Charles de Biron, the jilted fiancé, killed the Prince de Carency in a duel. Anne, a young widow of 12, was quickly remarried, this time to Jean des Cars' second son, Henri. Marguerite, who had never forgiven him for kidnapping her daughter, encouraged Geoffroy de Vivans to seek revenge. For his part, he placed his devotion to the family before his religious hatred, allied himself to the Duke of Mayenne, the Duke of Guise' brother, and laid siege to Vauguyon Castle where Anne was being held. She was again kidnapped and taken to Paris. As her second husband had died of illness, she was betrothed at the age of 18 to Mayenne's son, a little boy of 13. Four years later, she decided to marry somebody to her own taste. She faked a third kidnapping and married François d'Orléans-Longueville, Count of Saint-Pol, against her mother's advice.

LES MILANDES
9 miles S.W. of Sarlat

Les Milandes : the château that once belonged to Joséphine Baker.

Situated within the Castelnaud village boundaries, in the midst of a terraced park overlooking the left bank of the R. Dordogne, **Les Milandes Castle,** whose name remains for ever linked to that of **Joséphine Baker,** is **open to the public.** It was built c. 1489 by François de Caumont, lord of Castelnaud, and his wife, Claude de Cardaillac, who preferred to leave their austere fortress for a more pleasurable residence. After the last war, Les Milandes became the property of Joséphine Baker who founded her ''village of the world'' there, to look after abandoned children. Thanks to her, the sleepy village sprang back to life, as did the rest of the vicinity.

The castle is a pleasant transition from Gothic to Renaissance. The main building stands next to round and square towers with turrets on top. The dormer windows and mullioned bays topped by pinnacled pediments and decorated with coats-of-arms are very ornate.

41

Saint-Amand-De-Coly : a carved capital.

Saint-Amand-De-Coly : an arm of the transept.

The North of Dark Périgord : The Vézère Valley
ST.AMAND DE COLY
4 miles E. of Montignac

As soon as you get near the small village of St.Amand, the outline of a gigantic mass of stone is overwhelmingly visible. It is **the most beautiful fortified church in Périgord.** Legend has it that an abbey was founded there in the 7th century by **St. Amand,** an anachorete who evangelised Périgord. Although the **Romanesque abbey** was once of great importance as is obvious from the size of the buildings, it rapidly fell into decline. The redoubtable fortress was occupied by the Huguenots in 1575 and besieged by the Seneschal of Périgord and 2,000 soldiers who bombarded it with cannon fire for 6 days.

The church is still surrounded by **protective walls** topped by a parapet walk. After crossing the ramparts, visitors come face to face with a gigantic entrance **porch** which, from a distance, looks like a mouth ready to devour the entire village. The effect is lightened by a window and there is a ribbed arch supporting a **defensive chamber** that made it impossible to approach the gateway. Above the triple-arched doorway with capitals carved with foliage are twin atalantes dating from the Romanesque period. The walls in the south apse are decorated with appliques and the modillions on the cornice are adorned with carved heads and geometrical motifs. The apse, which is lit by three bays and a bulls' eye window, ends in a defensive terrace. The church's awesome defences are quite outstanding, the best preserved anywhere in Périgord. In addition to the outer wall and the belltower-keep, a **parapet walk** runs round the building beneath the roofs of stone slabs. On the corbels are corbelled **bartizans**. There are also defensive chambers on the crossings and the chevet, and three defensive positions at ground level near the chancel. This highly-elaborate system made it possible to keep the enemy at bay or to destroy it if it managed to get into the church. The plain, austere interior has all the **stark beauty** of Augustine abbeys. A **dome** on hanging keystones bearing traces of bullets tops the transept crossing. The south apsidal chapel contains **carvings** of an exceptionally high quality that are reminiscent of Souillac - two men eaten by a lion and a bird-dragon. The two spans in the chancel have very old ribbed vaulting.

MONTIGNAC-LASCAUX
16 miles N. of Sarlat

Montignac, a small town on the banks of the R. Vézère, with its population of 3,000, owes its fame to the discovery in 1940 of the "eighth wonder of the world" - the Lascaux cave.

It is difficult to imagine what **Montignac Castle**, the **military capital** of Périgord, looked liked when we see what remains today - a keep and a few pieces of wall that seem to have been eaten away by the village.

Montignac still has old houses around the parade ground. There is also the Périgord **Folk Museum** and the **Eugène Le Roy Museum** with a reconstitution of the writer's bedroom. **Eugène Le Roy** (1836-1907) was the greatest Périgord writer of all times and certainly the one who best translated, in a rough and engaging language, the charms of his local countryside and the hard living conditions of his fellows. His study of his century's misery made him, in some ways, the "Emile Zola of Périgord". Born in Hautefort, he went to school in Périgueux and was by then already a staunch Republican. He became a tax officer, which enabled him to travel around in his native region and to come to Montignac for the first time. He was appointed to Hautefort, where he published his first novel, *Le Moulin du Frau* (The Mill on the Frau) in 1893. Other works followed, including two with Montignac as their backcloth - *Mademoiselle de la Ralphie* and his masterpiece, *Jacquou le Croquant* which was published in 1900 and which Stellio Lorenzi brought into homes all over France in 1969 when he made it into a television serial. Eugène Le Roy retired to Montignac in 1902 where he wrote *Au pays des pierres, L'année rustique en Périgord* and his last novel published posthumously in 1911 and considered as one of his best, *L'ennemi de la Mort*. He was given a civil funeral, with a French flag draped over his coffin. Learning about Périgord through the writings of Eugène Le Roy means entering a world of country legends and daily misery made bearable by the great 19th-century hope of progress.

LASCAUX

One mile to the south is the most important stage of our trip through prehistory - the **Lascaux Cave**. Its chance discovery is like a fairytale. On 12th September 1940, four young lads decided to explore a dip in the Lascaux hillside. Legend had it that an underground passage containing a treasure trove linked this spot to Montignac Castle. They did indeed discover a treasure trove - the Lascaux cave, the most beautiful of all the decorated prehistoric caves. For many years, Lascaux' age was the subject of disagreement among experts. Prehistorians now generally believe that the paintings were done between the end of the Solutrean and the beginning of the Magdalanian Eras, i.e. some 15,000 years B.C. The Paleolithic artists found beneath the cave the three basic colours of the prehistoric palette - manganese dioxide (black), and ferrous oxides (reds and yellow ochres). Archaeological digs uncovered their lighting system - some one hundred tallow lamps. Three painting techniques were used - line-drawings done with fingers or crayons, "ragging" using tufts of hair or moss, and spraying on of paint using a hollow bone or a blowpipe.

Let us now go into the sanctuary. Entering the great hall of bulls is a memorable experience. A circle of animals seems to be moving - four huge bulls tower over horses and stags taking flight. All the animals seem to move as you go further into the chamber. The prehistoric artists regrouped them all on an imaginary ground halfway up the wall, and took advantage of every bump in the rock. A calcite chimney brings to life the expression on the face of a stag, a hump is used to emphasise the back of an animal or its belly or to bring out the muscles in its chest. The first painting in the chamber is already there in front of us, ready to pose us a problem. It has a panther's skin, a stag's tail, a bison's hump, and two horns. This is the famous unicorn, illustrated as being with young and having male sex organs. Is it an imaginary animal or, as some prehistorians have tenatively suggested, the "wizard" of Lascaux, as would seem

Lascaux II : "The Great Bull" ▶
in the Bull Chamber.

to be confirmed by the human legs and the face from which you merely have to remove the muzzle? Remember that where prehistory is concerned, any explanation is never more than mere hypothesis. Visitors then come upon four bulls. In fact, they are aurochs, a species which died out in France during the Middle Ages. The huge paintings (one of them measures almost 18 ft.) bring an impression of life and power to the chamber. This "presence" is achieved by the use of twisted perspective, an artistic effect which shows the animals from side view and their horns from three-quarters front. The technique, common throughout the Upper Paleolithic Period, is not the result of artistic incompetence but quite the reverse - it indicates the painters' great skill in depicting life.

Opposite the entrance is a narrow passage, the side corridor containing the finest paintings of all and the painted ceiling which won it the nickname forged by Father Breuil, "Prehistory's Sixtine Chapel". Here, the artists did not systematically attempt to achieve realism in their paintings. Instead, they created veritable compositions, like the "bouquet" of red cattle whose heads form a circle. The two main creatures in the corridor stand opposite each other - a powerful black bull reminiscent of Cretian art and a cow which appears to be jumping before a grid drawn at her feet. The horse is represented in various forms. The famous stylised "Chinese" horse enables us to appreciate the artists' technique more fully. The belly, which is partly covered in yellow ochre, is beginning to swell. In the middle distance, the legs detached from the rest of the body create the effect of perspective. This technique was not to be rediscovered until the Renaissance.

Come back into the great chamber and take the second corridor on your

"They are always there" ▶
(Le Thot).

Lascaux II : "The Great Black Bull" in the side passage.

◄*Lascaux II : "The Falling Cow" in the side passage. A frieze of small horses.*

left. It leads to the nave, a huge cavern in which the paintings have suffered more than elsewhere from the ravages of time. A large black cow dominates the scene because of its very massiveness, while two bison, remarkable for their savage denseness and blind fury, are shown running away as if surprised by the visitor's gaze. On the opposite side is a frieze of five stags, apparently swimming .This is a very gentle picture. A corridor that is rather difficult to reach leads to a small cave containing several engravings, in particular of cats. Finally, a hollow in the nave, the apse with its walls covered in numerous engravings, opens onto a well. Thirteen feet below at the bottom of the well is another enigma. What was the meaning of the wounded bison losing its entrails, the rhinoceros, the bird perched on a stick, and the naked man with the erect penis, all drawn in a childlike manner ?

Miraculously preserved by a layer of totally impermeable marl, Lascaux was doubly struck by illness brought in from outside by its visitors. First came a green leprosy, a proliferation of algae, then there was the white leprosy, the accelerated formation of calcite. In 1963, the cave was closed to the public. It was looked after like a bedridden patient, and has now regained its splendour. Yet it cannot risk opening its doors to the public again for fear of a relapse.

It took ten years' work to build the facsimile commissioned by Dordogne County Council. Using a computer, the cave was reconstructed to the nearest millimeter by Renaud Sanson. The paintings done using natural colours and prehistoric techniques were the work of Monique Peytral. The facsimile is a **masterpiece** in its own right. In fact, only an expert would know that he is not standing in the real cave. The entrance hall has been turned into a **museum.**

Three miles further west, on the edge of the Barade Forest, is the pretty Périgord village of **Fanlac** which became famous when **Stellio Lorenzi** situated the house of the good priest Bonal there during his filming of Jacquou le Croquant. Not far from the village is ''Combenegne'', the home of Eugène Le Roy's young hero. After the serial had been televised, veritable pilgrimages were made to the village. It is true that Fanlac has a certain charm with its well and its fortified Romanesque church. On the village square is a polylobed carved cross dating from the 17th century. The 14th- and 15th-century manorhouse was used as the home of the nobleman, de Galibert, in *Jacquou.*

Le Thot : a reconstitution of a prehistoric dwelling.

Thonac : the Château de Losse.

THONAC
4 miles S.W. of Montignac

The most outstanding feature of the village of Thonac is the church that houses a piece of sculpture unique in Périgord - a wooden **Romanesque statue of the Virgin Mary.**

Half-a-mile to the N is the **Le Thot Prehistoric Art Centre** which is **open to the public.** Built in 1972 by the good offices of the County Tourist Board, it is an excellent way of learning about prehistory. There is a zoo presenting "survivors" of prehisto-ric times - bison, tarpans, stags etc. The centre also has film and slide shows on artists' techniques in the Paleolithic Era and moulds of prehistoric objects.

Half-a-mile further north is **Losse Castle** which is **open to the public.** It stands in a quite **remarkable setting** on a short cliff containing a vast cave in which the architect dared to build a stone archway to support the terrace. At the foot of the rocks is the dark R. Vézère, providing a reflection of the castle. A 17th-century **barbican** stands at the entrance to the estate, roofed with stone slabs, well-protected, and preceded by a drawbridge adjacent to a curtain wall decorated witht turrets and pepper-pot watchtowers. The castle still has its moat and ramparts. After admiring the fine **façade** with its Renaissance windows, visitors enter the building by a magnificent stone staircase.

The best views of the wonderful countryside that includes the castles of Losse and Belcayre are to be had from the Montignac-Sergeac road along the left bank of the R. Vézère.

ST LEON SUR VEZERE
6 miles S.W. of Montignac

The road from Montignac to Les Eyzies skirts the beautiful little **village** of St. Léon without actually crossing it, but it is well worth a short stop. The site was occupied in ancient times - the church stands above **Gallo-Roman** foundations that can be clearly seen from the R. Vézère. The 11th-century **Romanesque church,** which is roofed with slabs, is dedicated to St. Léonce and was built in the shape of a cross. At the end is a barrel-vaulted apse flanked by two apsidal chapels. The apse is decorated with five supporting arches over columns with carved capitals. The vaulting in the apse and south apsidal chapel have frescoes from various periods. St. Léon's Church standing on a tiny, quietly-peaceful square, in its rustic setting on the banks of the river, is one of the oldest sanctuaries in Périgord. It was very skilfully restored in 1965. Its general **balance** and the perfect **harmony** of its chevet make it one of the most beautiful too. Take time to wander through the narrow alleys and between the old houses in the village which springs to life in the summer to the sound of the **Classical Music Festival.** On the edge of the road is **La Salle Castle,** standing proudly in the middle of a park. It consists of a square keep dating from the 14th century roofed with stone slabs. Behind it, the 16th-century **Clérans Manor** has tall roofs bearing weathervanes and pierced with dormer windows under pediments. The graveyard has 13th-century tombs and a very fine **expiatory chapel** built in the Gothic style and recently restored. The tympanum is decorated with a very strange inscription in Occitan, a reminder of the extraordinary events witnessed by the small community.

In the reign of St. Louis, in 1233 to be precise, a servant passed the graveyard and shot at the crucifix guarding the entrance with his crossbow. Blood gushed from the wound and the man fell stone dead with his head on back to front. So the legend goes, but is it really a **legend**? In 1890, the profaner's tomb was opened by members of the very worthy Périgord History and Archaeology Society. They found a skeleton with a skull facing the wrong way.

Saint-Léon-sur-Vézère : the perfect harmony of the chevet.

Sergeac : a capital in the doorway
to the Romanesque church.

Sergeac : the Hosanna Cross
at the crossroads.

SERGEAC-CASTELMERLE
6 miles S.W. of Montignac

Standing opposite the rocky spur topped by **Belcayre Castle**, the little **village** of Sergeac still has an unusually uniform appearance. Before reaching the village, there is a fine 15th-century wayside **Hosanna Cross** with carvings of Christ, the Virgin Mary, St. Michael, and a knight whose shield is covered with salamanders. This is an introduction to one of Périgord's major centres of cultural interest. A church built on a former Gallo-Roman estate existed as far back as 1053 ; it was part of the Sarlat diocese. The **Knights' Templar** set up a large commandery there in 1275 and it prospered rapidly. In 1280, Hélie Rudel, the powerful lord of Bergerac and Mon-

tignac, sold the Templars some land and his judicial rights over Sergeac. The monk-soldiers turned it into their **Grand Master**'s Périgord residence.

The slab-roofed houses of pale golden stone huddle round a 14th- and 15th-century manorhouse, once the residence of the Commander, a plain building with a round machicolated tower to one side and a fortified gateway. Half-a-mile from the village is a huge **walled enclosure** which serves as a reminder of where the commandery used to stand. In the heart of Sergeac, the starkness of the beautiful 12th-century Romanesque church shows the influence of the Knights Templar.

Like most of the villages in the Vézère Valley, Sergeac is of prehistoric importance. A few miles west of the village is the **Castelmerle Valley** containing rock shelters that are **open to the public.** The valley comes second only to Les Eyzies as the most densely-populated Paleolithic area in Dark Périgord. Its **nine rock shelters** were inhabited from 30,000 to 10,000 B.C. and have provided works of art and numerous tools. The **Blan-**

chard I shelter, which was occupied in the Aurignacian Era (30,000 to 25,000 B.C.), was discovered in 1910 and investigated by Breuil. It provided twenty blocks of stone bearing engravings of animals, some of them covered with paintings. There were also blocks showing rings and cupules. These works of art, which are among the oldest known to man, may be the remains of a mobile sanctuary. A dig was carried out on the **Labattut Shelter** in 1912 before it was investigated by Breuil and Glory. It was occupied in the Gravettian and Solutrean Periods. A child's skeleton dating from the Solutrean was found there. The shelter provided remains of paintings, two pebbles engraved with animals and blocks bearing engravings of rings, masterpieces from the Perigordian Period. The Reverdit Shelter discovered in 1878 was investigated by Breuil, Capitan and Peyrony. It contains a bas-relief of five animals carved in the Magdalanian Period. At the same time as you visit the Reverdit Shelter, you can see the **fortress-cave** also known as the "Englishmen's Cave".

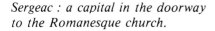

◀*Saint-Léon-sur-Vézère :
the interior of the church.*

PEYZAC LE MOUSTIER
6 miles N.E. of Les Eyzies

Peyzac and Le Moustier are two villages separated by the R. Vézère. Although there are several natural caves, it is **prehistory,** as omnipresent here as in Les Eyzies, which has made the village so well-known. The famous **Le Moustier Shelter,** which is **open to the public,** gave its name to the **Mousterian Era.** It consists of two shelters that were investigated in turn by Lartet in 1864 and by Peyrony. Each of them had elements of the Acheulian Mousterian as well of the characteristically Mousterian Era, covering a period from 100,000 to 35,000 B.C.. They also had traces of the Châtelperronian, a transitional period during which modern man first made his appearance, and of Early Aurignacian (30,000 B.C.). The second shelter contained the skeleton of a Neanderthal-type adolescent.

Half-a-mile to the west at the "Pas du Miroir" (Mirror's Step) where the road runs between the cliff face and the river and wends its way among the rocks, you can see one of the most outstanding sites in Périgord, standing high above the R. Vézère - **La Roque St. Christophe.** Five storeys, 260 ft. high and half-a-mile long, and a remarkable **fortress-cave** make this a "must" for prehistory and archaeology enthusiasts. The vast natural terrace, one of the largest anywhere in Europe, was inhabited back in the Mousterian Era (70,000 B.C.). It provided shelter in turn for Cro-Magnon Man, Stone Age Man, Bronze Age Man (15,000 B.C.) Iron Age Man (800 B.C.), the Gallo-Romans and the mediaeval population. The site open to visitors today is a gigantic set of cave dwellings that can be compared only to Capacdocce in Turkey. The fortress-cave was built by **Frotaire,** Bishop of Périgueux in the 10th century, to prevent the Vikings from sailing up the R. Vézère.

After crossing the original entry to the fort, you see rocks containing thousands of square **niches** which used to hold the supporting beams for the houses. The **shelters** contain recipients carved into the rock itself, pipes for the supply and drainage of

water, and **rings** carved into the rock (1,500 of them in all) to tie up animals and hang up lamps. Some of the chambers were built for set purposes (slaughterhouse, smoke curinghouse, strongbox). The village itself, suspended on five terraces, could accommodate between 1,000 and

La Roque-Saint-Christophe : the fortress-cave.

1,500 people. You can just imagine the hustle and bustle, the shops and the craft workshops. The **church** can still be picked out from the rest because of the engraved crosses and the tombs. From the terrace, there is a vast panoramic view of the R.Vézère.

Rouffignac :▶
the woolly rhınoceros, which
became extinct 10,000 years B.C..

Rouffignac : a mammoth and an ibex.

ROUFFIGNAC
10 miles N. of Les Eyzies

The village of Rouffignac, which was almost totally destroyed by the Germans on 31st March 1944, lies on the edge of the Barade Forest and was rebuilt after the war. All that remains intact of its past is the **Renaissance church.**

Three miles to the south, visitors can enjoy a marvellous **journey to the centre of the earth** by.taking a trip down to the **Cave of the One Hundred Mammoths.** No carbon lamps now as there were in Jules Verne's day ; instead a small **electric train** to take you through the cave.

The **huge cave** with more than 5 miles of galleries has never been closed and it has had visitors since the 16th century. Although it was explored by the famous prehistorians, Martel, Breuil, and Glory, its pain-

tings did not come to light until they were found in 1956 by Nougier and Robert. There were many who regarded the authenticity of the "find" with some scepticism at that time, but there are no doubts about them today. The cave was occupied fairly recently in prehistoric terms. The paintings date from the **Middle and Late Magdalanian,** i.e. 11,000 B.C. Digs carried out at the entrance showed that the cave was inhabited at the end of the prehistoric era (Tardenoisian, Sauveterrian, New Stone Age, and Iron Age).

Long before art existed, men must have fought **bears** for possession of these caverns. The sets and traces of claws show that the animals spent some time there. The first drawings are 800 yds. from the entrance and they continue right to the end of the galleries.

The cave gets its name from the **150 pictures of mammoths** that cons-

titute almost half of all known pictures of this type. It is strange to think that this mammoth sanctuary dates from a period in which the animal was already an endangered species in our regions, just like the woolly rhinoceros depicted on a frieze.

In some paintings, the mammoth is depicted in a very realistic fashion, e.g. the famous **"patriarch"** with its back marked with ritual signs. Often, though, only the outline is drawn. Near a well, the artist has illustrated the meeting of two herds. The small train stops at the entrance to the great hall whose painted **ceiling** of horses, bison, mountain goats, and mammoths is Rouffignac's masterpiece.

Three miles to the north is **L'Herm Castle** which is **open to the public** for those who are not afraid of meeting ghosts from a truly **Shakespearean drama.** A small path leads to the castle - little more than an **impressive** pile of ruins, apparently struck down by divine punishment.

In 1513, **Jean III de Calvimont,** future ambassador of François I, had the original fortress refurbished. The drama began with the violent and mysterious death of the son of L'Herm's builder who left his three-year-old daughter, **Marguerite,** to succeed him. His widow, **Anne d'Abzac,** acting more out of self-interest than for any sentimental reason, decided to marry Foucault d'Aubusson and lay hands on the inheritance at one and the same time. She therefore forced her daughter to marry Foucault's son, François. Years passed without bringing any happiness to the forced marriage. François fell in love with one **Marie d'Hautefort,** the aunt of Louis XIII's mistress, Aurore. He then had only one idea in his mind - to rid himself of Marguerite. Apparently, he had his mother-in-law's complicity in this macabre project. One day in February 1605, he gave all his servants the day off, forced Marguerite to sign a letter divesting her of all her wealth and had her strangled.

But François did not get off so lightly. An autopsy was requested and statements poured in. Overcome with panic if not with remorse, Anne d'Abzac accused her son-in-law of murdering her daughter. Thereafter, François never travelled without a troop of armed men, and they promptly killed the soldiers sent to arrest him. The case was at a standstill and, in 1606 while still a free man, François married Marie d'Hautefort.

Three years after the murder, Anne d'Abzac was persuaded, again out of self-interest, to withdraw her claim to part of her daughter's inheritance. But those around her, in particular the **Calvimonts** de Saint Martial, caused a scandal and forced her to prosecute the assassin. François d'Aubusson gave himself up in Paris and died in the Conciergerie a few years later.

Unfortunately, things did not stop there. Marie d'Hautefort proved to be as hard a character as Anne d'Abzac. After arranging the murder of the two Saint Martial brothers, she obtained legal rights to the ownership of the castle. But bloodshed brings more bloodshed in its wake and her son, Charles, was murdered in his turn. In an attempt to provide herself with some measure of protection, Marie married **Raphaël de Baudet,** a former accomplice.

Re-enacting an earlier scene from the drama, she betrothed her daughter, Françoise, to her husband's son. But Françoise was already engaged to Godefroy de la Roche-Aymon. The two fiancés fought a duel and contrary to all expectations Godefroy killed his enemy. When he became a member of the family, he also entered his mother-in-law's service by killing, in another duel, a Calvimont who had dared to marry the widow of Marie's murdered son.

In 1641, Françoise died in childbed. Marie's wicked advisor, Raphaël de Baudet, had Charles de Chaumont murdered - a brother-in-law with whom she had quarrelled. But he himself died in the shoot-out that he had organised. Years passed, all of them as dark as their predecessors. Françoise' daughter lost her first husband during the war ; the second one was murdered. As for Marie d'Hautefort, she died a fine death in 1652 in the accursed castle. L'Herm was finally purchased in 1682 by another Marie d'Hautefort who left sweeter memories, and rented out to a farmer.

Rouffignac : the ruins of l'Herm Castle. If only stones could speak !

TURSAC-LA MADELEINE
3 miles N.E. of Les Eyzies

Apart from its 12th-century fortified Romanesque church with the
belltower-keep and line of domes,
and its carved stone cross, the tiny
village of Tursac would be of little
interest if it were not one of Périgord's main centres of prehistory.
Opposite the village, on the right
bank of the R. Vézère at the water's
edge, is the great **Madeleine Shelter,**
which gave its name to the Magdalanian Period and which is now a
charming and rustic place for a
stroll. The digs from 1863 onwards,
carried out by Lartet and later by
Peyrony, uncovered numerous tools,
some fine specimens of furnishings
and a child's skeleton. More importantly, though, the digs enabled
experts to establish the whole chronology of the Middle and Upper
Magdalanian, for the site had been
occupied right up until the Azilian
Era, i.e. from 12,000 to 8,000 B.C.

The prehistoric part of La Madeleine is not open to the public but the
fortress-cave and the remains of the
castle are well worth a visit. Here, as
in many places in Périgord, an early
mediaeval village (10th century) was
established on the same site as a prehistoric settlement, dug into the rock
and fortified to resist attack from the
Vikings. In this huge troglodyte village, which was still inhabited in the
17th century, note the 15th-century
chapel said by legend to contain a
treasure trove, and a watchtower
many feet up in the air. These watchtowers enabled guards to communi-
cate from one fortress to another
using lights and to seek assistance in
case of attack. Visitors see, among
other things, the village's defensive
system and the day-to-day life of our
cave-dwelling ancestors. On top of
the hill is the mediaeval castle of **Le
Petit Marzac,** the third "storey" in
this outstanding example of the eter-
nity of life over the centuries and the
millenia.

*Tursac : part of the La Madeleine
fortress-cave.*

Les Eyzies : the cliffs full of shelters and cave-dwellings.

*Les Eyzies : the cliffs hide the Potholing ▶
Museum and the Grand Roc Cave.*

LES EYZIES
13 miles W. of Sarlat

It is commonplace to describe Les Eyzies as the capital of prehistory. The numerous decorated caves and multiplicity of rock shelters merely confirm the idea. A wide variety of styles and periods of both prehistory and history are represented here, making Les Eyzies the archetypal **time-machine village.** A long, statio-nary walk will illustrate the passage of time in the prehistoric period - from La Micoque to Laugerie-Basse, from 200,000 to 5,000 years B.C.. Prehistory in Les Eyzies has lasted forty times longer than history, and one hundred times longer than Christianity.

Even if prehistory were not there, present with every step, Les Eyzies would be worth a visit for its setting. Standing at the confluence of the rivers Vézère and Beune, the little village dominated by an old castle that has become a museum hangs grimly on beneath tall cliffs full of shelters, caves and **cave dwellings,** beneath green oaks and juniper bushes. After crossing the R. Vézère, a narrow road picks its way between the river and the wall of rock, following the "royal progress" of prehistory - an unimaginable succession of caves and shelters in an impressive landscape of cliffs.

Les Eyzies, the museum esplanade : Neanderthal Man by the sculptor, Dardé.

The National Prehistory Museum

The **castle** in Les Eyzies, which was purchased by the State in 1913 with the encouragement of Peyrony, is itself built over the top of a prehistoric site and a village of cave dwellings. It became the Prehistory Museum in 1918. Nowadays, its collections include almost one million items. The clarity of the presentation and the wide range of treasures it contains make it an easy and fascinating museum for visitors. They start on the third floor of the keep with the "land of hewn stone" presented in chronological order. The second floor of the keep is devoted mainly to art. The first floor houses maps, and chronological and explanatory tables. On the ground floor, the Renaissance building houses a summary of the first discoveries, the methods employed during archaeological digs, and the description of a few sites.

Before leaving, take a look at the splendid panoramic view from the terrace and do not forget to doff your cap at the museum's stone guardian, the famous "primitive man". But do not make the usual mistake of confusing him with "Cro-Magnon" - he might be annoyed.

The decorated caves

FONT DE GAUME : On the Sarlat road on the outskirts of Les Eyzies, a steep path up the side of the cliff then a narrow entrance that would be perfect as an illustration for one of Jules Verne's novels or a Walt Disney film takes us to Font de Gaume. The cave, which is **open to the public,** has a fine set of **engravings** and polychrome paintings, **most of them dating from the Magdalanian Period** (12,000 B.C.). Sixty-five yards in from the cave mouth, the corridor narrows. This is the "Rubicon", the start of the decorated section. It is indicated by red dots

Les Eyzies, Font-de-Gaume : a reindeer and bison at the junction of the main gallery and the side passage.

Les Eyzies, Font-de-Gaume : a horse partially covered with calcite.

*Les Eyzies where life is an unending chain :
prehistoric watchtowers and fortress caves.*

on the wall. A series of lines indicates the end of the gallery. Once we have passed the "Rubicon", we come face to face with the first frieze - a dozen mammoths and bison. A combination of engraving and painting. Further on, near the junction on the left-hand side, is the famous painting of **reindeer confronting each other.** A large male is bending over a female with legs bent. On the right, in the side gallery, there are several bison, reindeer and horses, but they have been partly damaged by calcite. Back in the main gallery, a large frieze showing five engraved and painted bison stands out against a background of white calcite. At the end of the gallery in a recess known as the Bison Chapel, are four polychrome bison among the dozen or so paintings.

LES COMBARELLES

Discovered in 1901 and investigated by Capitan, Breuil and Peyrony, the Combarelles cave, which is also **open to the public** is near the Sarlat road, a mile from Font-de-Gaume. Some **800 engravings** cover the 270 yds. of winding underground passages. On the walls of the last 75 yds., there is a multiplicity of intermingled engravings - mammoths, ibex, wild asses, bears, reindeer, woolly rhinoceros, bison and horses. The horse theme is noticeably predominant with almost 140 distinct engravings. They date from the Middle and Late Magdalanian (12,000 to 10,000 B.C.). The cave is also famous for its many human figures, 48 of them in all. Among the other items of note in the cave is the engraving of a lio-

ness, ass and ibex, one of the rare paintings in Les Combarelles. More striking still is the engraving of a reindeer bending down to drink. In many cases the engravings are incomplete and visitors can let their imaginations run riot amidst the network of lines and symbols, seeing different things depending on the angle of the light.

Just over a mile from Les Eyzies is **La Mouthe Cave,** discovered in 1891. It has been closed to the public since 1981 in an effort to avoid damage. It will not open its doors again unless the works of art that it contains (engravings outlined in yellow ochre) are no longer in danger. The engravings date from the **Gravettian** (25,000 B.C.) to the **Late Magdalanian** (10,000 B.C.). The main attraction is still the painted

engravings of what is believed to be a prehistoric **hut.**

THE SHELTERS

We shall now look at the main shelters occupied in prehistoric times by the tribes around Les Eyzies, taking them in chronological order so that they show some semblance of continuity.

The **Micoque** site is not content with giving its name to the Micoquian, an industry existing simultaneously with the beginning of the Mousterian in 100,000 B.C. Its lowest level provided flints that were much older, dating from **200,000 years** ago, worked by the first inhabitants of Les Eyzies.

It was, though, in the Aurignacian (30,000 B.C.) with the arrival of Homo Sapiens Sapiens that Les Eyzies and the surrounding area underwent a veritable population explosion and became the centre of the prehistoric world. The race from the Aurignacian Period which chose Périgord as the place to live and create the earliest works of art, is better-known to us as **Cro-Magnon Man.** It was in the Cro-Magnon rock shelter near the hotel of the same name that five skeletons were discovered in 1868, surrounded by jewellery and shells. Lartet's study of the finds enabled him to define a tall race of human beings (approx. 6 ft.) resembling us both in physique and cranial capacity.

The Gorge d'Enfer (Hell's Gorge), which is **open to the public,** has several small caves and one gigantic rock shelter.

Still in Hell's Gorge, the **Fish Shelter** has a first, Aurignacian, level but the **carving of a large salmon** on the ceiling dates from the Gravettian (25,000 B.C.) or Early Perigordian (30,000 B.C.).

The 14 archaeological layers in the **Pataud Shelter** cover the Aurignacian, Gravettian and Early Solutrean Periods (32,000 to 18,000 B.C.). The cave contains a wall engraving of a **female figure.** Thanks to the encouragement of Henri de Lumley, a **site museum** is due to open shortly.

Laugerie-Haute, which is **open to the public,** has been used as the basis of prehistoric chronology because of its 42 layers of rock. Occupied at the end of the Gravettian 20,000 years B.C., it is more typical of the Solutrean Period (20,000 to 15,000 B.C.) of which it contains all the stratigra-

Les Combarelles : the "drinking" reindeer.

◀*Les Combarelles : an engraving of a horse's head.*

Les Eyzies, Font-de-Gaume :▶
two remarkable specimens of the great Bison Frieze.

phic series. It was abandoned in the Magdalanian after the collapse of its uppermost terrace in approx. 14,000 B.C.

The first shelter on the **Laugerie-Basse** site, which is **open to the public,** contained a large quantity of implements dating from the Middle Upper Magdalanian and Azilian Periods i.e. between 12,000 and 8,000 B.C. Lartet carried out a dig there in 1864. In 1872, a skeleton was uncovered, surrounded by shells. The second shelter, the Marseilles, dates from a longer period. The

entire Magdalanian from 15,000 to 10,000 B.C. is present here.

Let us leave prehistory on one side and turn to history instead, to visit **Tayac Church** which was built as a **fortress** by the monks of Paunat Abbey in the 12th century.

On the other bank of the R. Vézère, the **Tayac Rock** was originally a **fortress-cave** before becoming a fortress and tollgate for river traffic in the Late Middle Ages. At the turn of the century, it was turned into an "aerial restaurant" but now houses the **Pot-Holing Museum.** Its

collections include specialist equipment, specimens of cave-dwelling fauna, and explanatory tables.

Among the prehistoric sites above Laugerie-Basse, the **Gran Roc Cave** is open to the public. It is filled with stalagmites and stalactites. Discovered in 1924, it has some fine "eccentrics" resembling coral.

Manaurie on the Périgueux road beyond Laugerie-Haute has another such cave, which is also open to the public. This is **Carpe Diem,** a cave with coloured stalagtites.

SIREUIL-COMMARQUE
4 miles E. of Les Eyzies

Above the valleys of the two **Beune rivers** that flow into the R. Vézère is the little village of **Sireuil** which still has its 12th-century Romanesque domed church. It also has some large **prehistoric sites** (but then we are not far from Les Eyzies). But Sireuil is particularly well-known for the Permanent Centre for Basic Environmental Studies (C.P.I.E) which organises a large number of courses, mainly on historical and ecological topics.

Around the village are some remarkable **bories,** or stone huts. The most famous bories in Périgord, the **"Le Breuil Gallic huts"** are some 4 miles S.E. of Sireuil near the tiny hamlet of Bénivès. Built near a farm and used as sheep-pens, they form a strange group of buildings. Nobody has ever proved the reason for their being called "Gallic"; this type of hut could just as well have been built 3,000 years B.C. as during the last century. The **film industry** could hardly ignore such a setting. Stellio Lorenzi's *Jacquou le Croquant* and Robert Hossein's *Les Misérables* both contain sequences featuring these picturesque bories, places that are likely to remain an irritating archaeological mystery for many years to come.

Three miles E of Sireuil on a fairly inaccessible site isolated from nearby hamlets by a dense forest, **Commarque** seems to be a phantom castle, standing guard over a marshy valley crossed by the R. Beune. It was once a perfect example of a Périgord mediaeval **fortress** but is now no more than a vast **ruin** overrun but a short time ago by undergrowth and trees. its tall keep towers high above the remainder of a village that was originally protected by gigantic ramparts. Time seems to have stood still here, and visitors often have a feeling of oppressive leadenness.

The site was occupied way back in the mists of time. Underneath the castle is a **prehistoric cave.** It contains a carved horse reminiscent of its "neighbours" in Cap Blanc. The **cliff** between the cave and the enormous 13th-century castle is filled with a network of shelters, the remains of a **fortress-cave** probably cut into the rock in the 9th or 10th century. This succession of dwellings is like a long slice of man's history fixed in time some 500 years ago. It is striking and rather frightening. What do we know of its history?

At the beginning of the 12th century, Gérard de Commarque gave his wealth to the **Knights Templar.** The castle became a commandery which, after the tragic disappearance of the Order, passed to the Knights Hospitaller of St. John of Jerusalem. They erected the enormous **keep** then sold the castle to the Baron of Beynac. After the Treaty of Brétigny (1360), the lord of Commarque, like his cousin Beynac, rallied to Charles V's cause and put up resistance against the invader.

In 1370, Pons de Beynac died, leaving as his sole heiress a little girl aged three - Philippa. Her inheritance was under threat from her neighbour and rival, Castelnaud, who supported the English camp. In order to ensure her protection, **Pons de Commarque,** who was then in the prime of life, became engaged to the child. He did battle for France, became the master of almost the whole of Dark Périgord, and married Philippa in 1379 when she was 12. It seems that the young mistress of Commarque was not to live long for, in 1405, Pons was married for a second time - to Magne de Castelnaud. Through his two marriages, he allied himself to the most powerful lords in the Dordogne Valley - Beynac and Castelnaud.

Yet in 1406, Commarque was invaded by Archambaud d'Abzac's troops. Pons and his family remained prisoners of the English for six months until their freedom was paid for. In gratitude for services rendered, King Charles VII gave him Campagne Castle. He died in 1440. His successors lacked his wisdom. Throughout the 15th and 16th centuries, they pillaged the vicinity and ransomed travellers, thereby giving the castle its sinister reputation.

The castle is now once again the

property of the Commarque family and its owner, although wishing to slow down the building's decline, wants to maintain its wild, romantic

Sireuil : Commarque Castle and the tall keep built by the Knights Templar.

character and leave visitors to wander at will. After crossing the two drawbridges over the dry moat protected by barbicans, visitors see a 13th-16th century building with mullioned windows, bristling with staircase towers. Visitors stroll through the devastated rooms with yawning fireplaces, before climbing the huge, square 12th-century keep from which there is a breathtaking panoramic view, an Alpha and Omega land-

Commarque and its "little brother", Laussel.

▲*Commarque : the ruined interior.*

◄*Commarque :
the remains of the chapel.*

scape where vegetation and rocks seem to have agreed to shut out every sign of human existence. At the foot of the castle is the mediaeval **village** where you can still make out the Romanesque church and its crypt and the bread oven in a tumbledown house. Opposite stands **Laussel**, the elegant "younger brother" in the Beune Valley, a vital complement to Commarque if the setting is to work all its charm. Between the castles is the **marshy plain** once covered with flax, that now hides its terrible, muddy mantraps. The clear waters of the Beune flow through the middle. The countryside preserved from the passage of time and the blackest type of romanticism could hardly avoid firing artistic imaginations. Robert Merle situated the action of his book, *Malevil,* there and Claude Cénac his novel, *Demain l'an mil.* As for the film director Ridley Scott, he filmed the wonderful ending of his *Dualists* here.

Cap-Blanc : part of the frieze.

Marquay : the chevet.

MARQUAY
7 miles N.W. of Sarlat

Perched on a hilltop between the two Beune rivers, the tiny village of Marquay gathers its beautiful Périgord houses around its 12th- and 13th -century fortified **Romanesque church.**

Three miles to the west, a visit to the **Cap Blanc Shelter** is an unforgettable experience. The shelter has one of the most impressive prehistoric friezes anywhere in the world. Along a length of more than 42 ft. are deeply-scored **carvings** of **horses** and cattle which seem about to spring out of the rock face. Their size (the central haut-relief of a horse is 7 ft. long) and artistic qualities give the frieze a striking realism. The work probably dates from the Early or Middle Magdalanian (13,000 B.C.).

Three miles to the west, above the Geun Marshes opposite the formidable fortress of Commarque, is the 15th- and 16th-century **Laussel Castle** which, although it has undergone major restoration, is an elegant building with machicolated towers, a square keep, and a 17th-century chapel. Near the castle are a strange **troglodyte dovecot** and the famous **prehistoric site of Laussel.** It contains the famous "Venus of Laussel" carved in a golden-yellow stone.

Three miles to the south near Sarlat, the elegant outline of **Puymartin** rises above the trees in the forest. Built in the 15th and 16th centuries and restored in the 20th, it is **open to the public** and houses an interesting collection of old furniture.

Marquay : Laussel Castle seen from Commarque.

LE BUGUE
7 miles W. of Les Eyzies

Surrounded by wooded hills, and built up in terraces above the right bank of a meander of the R. Vézère, the friendly little town of Le Bugue (prehistory's Golden Gate) is one of the largest communities in Dark Périgord, with 3,000 inhabitants.

Half-a-mile to the N.W. is the **Bara-Bahau Cave** discovered in 1951 by the pot-holer Norbert Casteret. This 325 ft. long cavity is **open to the public.** On the very soft, crumbly rock (Father Glory compared it to cottage cheese), prehistoric artists engraved mysterious roof-shaped signs and outlines of aurochs, bears, bison, ibex and horses with their fingers, flints or stick. Because of the very rustic style of the work, it is difficult to date. Father Breuil saw it as being the first steps in art. Nowadays, it is thought to date from the **early Magdalian** (15,000 B.C.).

The **Proumeyssac Swallow-hole,** 3 miles to the S., is **open to the public.** There is an **aven with rock formations** over 160 ft. high, a large number of translucid stalactites (that are still alive thanks to a stream running through the cave), strange-shaped "eccentrics", a petrified fountain and some very unusual triangular cristallisations.

Three miles to the E. is the tiny village of **St Cirq du Bugue** which has a **prehistoric cave** that is **open to the public.** It boasts an outstanding **engraving of a man** with a complete human face. At the same time as visitors see the prehistoric cave, they can also take a look of the **fortress-cave** of Le Pech Saint-Sourd.

Le Bugue : a very rare engraving of a bear in Bara-Bahau.

The fortified villages

CADOUIN
26 miles S.W. of Sarlat

The village of Cadouin with its old houses and covered market grew up in the shadow of its **abbey,** founded in 1115 in the depths of the Bessede Forest by Robert d'Arbrissel, with the backing of Géraud de Sales. But the abbey's prosperity was based on a prestigious relic brought back from Antioch and mentioned in 1117 as being in Cadouin - the **Holy Shroud** that was wrapped around Christ's head.

It was hung in a silver reliquary from the church roof and became the object of a major **pilgrimage** which brought together rich and poor alike. After all, was it not seen by Eleanor of Aquitaine, Richard the Lionheart, St. Louis, Blanche of Castille, and Charles V ? Thanks to Louis XI, the abbey was renovated and given the splendid Gothic cloisters that can still be seen today. When the abbey became part of the commendatory system, it fell into a spiritual decline but remained a busy centre of pilgrimage. Rabelais, during a visit to Périgord where he had many friends, visited Cadouin and mentioned the Holy Shroud in his book, *Gargantua*. During the French Revolution, the last monks were expelled. Yet in the 19th century, pilgrimages began again. Once more, crowds assembled to attend solemn ceremonies and the trade in medals, crucifixes and pious images flourished. In 1925, the first doubts were expressed as to the authenticity of the Holy Shroud by Reverend Father Francez. An

A rent in a veil of mist, an eternal landscape of the beginnings of mankind.▶
"France may one day cease to exist but Périgord will survive,
like the dreams that feed the human soul". (Henry Miller).

Cadouin : the Gothic cloisters.

enquiry ordered in 1932 by church authorities revealed that the fabric, although of oriental origin, bore a Kufic inscription in praise of Allah dating from the 11th century. Cadouin's Holy Shroud was a **fake.**

The **Romanesque church** was consecrated in 1154. Its wide West front divided in three by piers is made lighter by a triple-arched doorway topped by a row of blind arching. Its austerity, which is typical of **Cistercian** churches, is tempered by the beautiful golden Périgord stone and by the carvings on the outer pillars and the modillions round the cornice. Inside, there are three barrel-vaulted aisles, a dome on hanging keystones over the transept crossing, and barrel-vaulted apsidal chapels. Although the cloisters in Cadouin were damaged during the Wars of Religion and the French Revolution, they remain a masterpiece of religious architecture with their richly-decorated vaulting and pillars. Work began in the 15th century with the assistance of King Louis XI, and was completed in the 16th century. The west gallery is decorated with remarkable Renaissance **carvings.** Among the Biblical themes (the stories of Job, Lazarus, and Samson and Delilah) are lay themes (satirical and popular scenes reminiscent of Flemish paintings, and illustrations of fables). The vaulting has a Last Judgement, Abraham's sacrifice, and the Flight into Egypt. It also bears the remains of 15th-century frescoes. In the north gallery fitted into the stone are the monks' benches, the reader's seat, and the abbot's chair. To each side of the abbot's seat are two carved pillars representing the walk to Calvary and a procession.

The Le Blanc passage grave in the parish of Nojals-et-Clotte near Beaumont.

Beaumont : the fortified church.

BEAUMONT du PERIGORD
18 miles S.E. of Bergerac

The **fortified village** of Beaumont founded in 1272 now reigns peacefully over a rather sleepy stretch of countryside. Yet in the Middle Ages, it was one of the largest fortified villages in Périgord. The Seneschal of Guyenne, Lucas de Thaney, presided over its creation on behalf of the King of England, Edward I, who called it his "first royal fortified village". It was not built on a square as was customary in those days but in the shape of an 'H' in memory of his father Henry III. It was not completely freed from English domination until after the Battle of Castillon (1453).

Beaumont has lost some of its original character, unlike Domme or Monpazier. But the village's main attraction is undoubtedly **St. Front's Church,** one of the finest **military Gothic** churches in Périgord. The vast, austere building was first designed for defensive purposes for, unlike most of the fortified villages, Beaumont had no castle. The four towers connected by a parapet walk look more like keeps than belltowers. The carved Gothic doorway with a balcony and frieze of human figures over it has a certain elegance.

Monpazier : the main square within the walled town.

MONPAZIER
31 miles S.W. of Sarlat

Built above the Dropt Valley not far from the source of the river, **Monpazier** is certainly the most beautiful and best-preserved of all Périgord's **English fortified villages.** Along with the villages of Beaumont, Molières, Lalinde and Fonroque, to which should be added the unsuccessful attempts at such villages in Pépicou, Roquépine, Castelréal, Puyguilhem, Beaulieu and Labastide, it was part of the English defensive system for South Périgord. Today, Monpazier is one of smallest villages in France (43 hectares) but it still has its north- and south-facing **checkerboard layout** measuring 433 yds. by 238 yds. ringed by ramparts. The streets set at right angles to each other are subdivided by a network of alleyways. At the heart of the village is the main square surrounded on all sides by houses with **arcades.**

Edward I, King of England, Duke of Aquitaine, decided to found Monpazier by an act dated 7th January 1284. The village was founded by **Jean de Grailly,** Seneschal of Périgord for King Edward I of England who came to visit the village in person in 1286. The population enjoyed a number of advantages such as exemption from taxes and abolition of seigniorial rights. In spite of this, the village proved difficult to establish. The king had to threaten a 10-livre fine for any inhabitant who refused to build his house as required. The consuls elected to govern the village also had problems with their neighbour, Aymeric de Biron, Lord of Montferrand. Some of his serfs had run away and sought refuge in the village where they had gained their freedom in accordance with the charter. During the One Hundred Years' War, Monpazier changed hands several times. After a century of peace, the area was ravaged by the Wars of Religion and, on 21st June 1574, the village was captured by the Huguenot captain, **Geoffroy de Vivans,** as a result of an act of treachery. Monpazier was also the general headquarters of the peasant revolutionaries who held an assembly there on 22nd May 1594. After numerous attacks on castles, the troubles died down in 1597. A new revolt in 1637 brought 8,000 peasants together under the leadership of **Buffarot,** a weaver from the nearby village of Capdrot. He was taken prisoner and drawn and quartered on 16th August 1637 on Monpazier's main square. On 1st June 1879, Monpazier was the birthplace of **Jean Galmot,** journalist, writer and author of two best-sellers, *Quelle étrange histoire* and *Un mort vivait parmi nous.* But most of all, he was an adventurer.

His friend, **Blaise Cendrars,** wrote a book about him called *Rhum* in which he described Monpazier as a "tiny island of stones, of very old stones....a geometrical town laid out like an American community."

Monpazier has retained its Gothic character. Today, fairs are still held on the day fixed by the charter. The main square still has its mediaeval appearance. It is surrounded by arcades that are also known as "valleys" or "covers" for they form a covered

Monpazier : the arcades.

Monpazier : the covered market.

walkway where people can shelter from the rain and the sun. The houses round the square are all the same size - 26 ft. wide and 65 ft. deep. They are separated by narrow alleys that served as firebreaks and rubbish heaps. On the square, the 16th-century **covered market** still has its old grain scales. In one corner is the well. Three **fortified gates** out of the original six in the town walls are still standing - one on the south side and two to the north topped by circular towers. On the west side is a postern gate, the ''Gateway to Paradise''. The chapter house near the church (13th-14th centuries), formerly a tithe barn, has twin windows on all three floors. The West Front of the **Gothic church** built in the 13th and 14th centuries was rebuilt in 1550. In the chancel, the beautiful stalls dating from 1492 are carved with creatures from a fantasy world or grotesque figures.

BIRON
36 miles S.E. of Sarlat

Four miles S.W. of the splendid fortified village of Monpazier, on the borders of Périgord and the Agen region, is the **largest castle** in the county. The enormous mass of this Périgord **barony** keeps watch over 19 miles of surrounding countryside. It was a rare, if not unique, example of a family estate - twenty-four generations of Gontauts owned the castle from the 12th century to 1938. The continuity produced a harmonious, though diverse, set of buildings despite a blend of architectural styles and the ups and downs of history. In 1189, Gaston de Gontaut married his daughter, Raymonde, to the **Cathar Martin d'Algaïs,** Lord of Bigaroque, Seneschal of Gascony and Périgord for the King of England. The crusade preached by St. Dominic brought fire and bloodshed to the south-west and the Cathar forces took shelter in Biron in 1211 where they were besieged by Simon de Montfort. He agreed to spare everybody's life if the defendents gave Martin d'Algaïs up

Biron : the castle and private chapel.

to him. The Cathar was dragged along behind a horse then hung.

The lineage of the illustrious Gontaut family was not interrupted by the Wars of Religion. They remained Catholic while at the same time providing accommodation for the Queen of Navarre and the Prince of Condé. **Armand de Gontaut-Biron,** Henri IV's companion made Mars- hal of France in 1576, fought at Evry and Arques before being killed at the Siege of Epernay in 1592. Brantôme, who knew a fine soldier when he saw one, nicknamed him "France's greatest captain".

His son, **Charles de Gontaut** (1562-1602) inherited his fiery temperament. Henri IV adored him, calling him "the most trenchant instru- ment of my victories". The king covered the young man with honours, making him an admiral, Marshal of France in 1595, Lieutenant General of the Armed Forces, Duke and Peer of France in 1598, and Governor of Burgundy. But his ambition was to be his downfall. With the Duke of Savoy and the Spanish Governor of Milan, he plotted

Biron : one of the towers.

difficult to understand visually as they are mentally. No description can really do justice to the intermingled mass of architectural styles and carvings. Jean Secret distinguished between three buildings.

Visitors enter the castle by a square tower with a 13th-century base. The remainder was altered in the 15th and 16th centuries. The barbican, which has a decorated gate and dormer window, leads into the first courtyard. Next to the tower at the entrance is a Renaissance **loggia** leading to the **collegiate chapel.** This is the finest section of the castle. Built on two floors, it has two naves, one above the other. The ground floor looks out onto the village and was used as a parish church. The upper storey looks onto the castle and was the family chapel. With its ogival vaulting, it is a pleasant blend of Flamboyant Gothic and Renaissance architecture. It contains richly-carved tombs with recumbent figures of those responsible for the rebuilding of the chapel and the restoration of the castle - Pons de Gontaut, who died in 1524, and his brother Armand, Bishop of Sarlat, who died in 1531.

Isolated on the north side of the lower courtyard is a small 14th-century manorhouse with vaulting decorated with 16th-century frescoes. This was the tax office to which peasants came to pay their tithes. Symmetrically opposite this building, and dating from the same period, is the round St. Peter Tower.

After climbing a 17th-century staircase and going through a Renaissance gateway, you enter the **main courtyard.** The old 12th-century keep is an impressive piece of work, while a building from the Renaissance and 17th century housing the States General Chamber built in the early part of the 17th century by Marshal de Biron is slightly overwhelming because of its sheer size. At the end of the courtyard, a 17th-century **peristyle** of slim columns opens onto a pleasant rustic landscape. The visit ends with the Marshal's Pavilion and by a visit "below stairs" to the castle's vast kitchens.

to dismember the kingdom, thereby acquiring Aquitaine for himself. The king forgave him. He again became involved in a plot and fomented revolt. The king would have pardonned him again if he had owned up to his misdeeds but he refused. He was beheaded on 31st July 1602 in the Bastille. The king was loath indeed to cut himself off from a person who, in his own words, could "no more help saying ill of others than doing good when he had his backside in the saddle and a sword in his hand."

Biron has belonged to the County of Dordogne since 1978 and is **open to the public.** But you will not see just one castle. It is a group of castles from different periods that are as

Hautefort : the château and its moat.

Hautefort : the façade and barbican.▶

Central Périgord
HAUTEFORT
19 miles N. of Montignac

Hautefort Castle can be seen from miles away. Its **"17th-century"** style comes as rather a surprise in this area of France. Perched on a hilltop between the R. Bauze and the R. Lourde, it has the haughty geographical position of a mediaeval fortress and the perfect balance of 17th-century buildings.

After crossing the drawbridge, visitors enter the castle by a barbican flanked by two lookout towers dating from 1588. Opposite are two main buildings preceded by two wings ending in two round **towers** topped by **bell turrets.** The main building is flanked by domed pavilions and framed by two more pavilions dating from the 18th century. The perfect **symmetry** is further emphasised by the harmonious well-balanced slate roof. A main staircase connects the first floor and ground floor which has a beautiful arcaded gallery with basket-handle arching. The interior is richly-furnished. In the west tower with its fine rafters, there is a collection of craft objects and a reminder of **Eugène Le Roy's books** (he was born in the castle in 1836). But Hautefort's finest treasure is perhaps its 30-hectare park containing a variety of trees and **formal gardens** with a blend of flowerbeds, box hedges, and paths roofed over with thuyas. It is a very pleasant place for a stroll, in the shadow of the great people who lived here in times past.

Bertran de Born (1150-1214) was, with his contemporary Bernard de Ventadour, the most famous **troubadour** of the Occitan language. He may have sung the praises of womanhood and described the life in noble courts but do not imagine him with a lovelorn look in his eye and his lute under his arm. Although he travelled from one castle to another like all good troubadours, it was so that he could take them by storm for Bertran de Born was first and foremost a formidable warlord, a **"sower of discord"**. Dante's expression,

which took the poet straight to Hell in the "Divine Comedy", is a perfect description. After robbing his brother of his share of the inheritance, he became involved in the Plantagenets' quarrels. His castle was besieged five times. As Richard the Lionheart's enemy, he encouraged Richard's brother Henry Shortmantel to rebel against his father, King Henry II of England. His hopes were dashed when Henry Shortmantel died suddenly and he wept for him with absolute sincerity, "if all the tears, misfortunes and miseries of this painful century were brought together, they would seem but little compared to the death of the young English king". Worn out by an eventful life, Bertran de Born retired in 1196 to the neighbouring abbey of **Dalon** where he died c. 1214.

Jacques François d'Hautefort, who was born in 1610 and who distinguished himself at the Battle of Rocroi (1643), gave Hautefort the appearance it still has today. He is said to have been very miserly and Molière is thought to have based his character Harpagon on him. The Marquise de Sévigné related his death in 1650 as follows, "He never wanted to take any English remedy, saying that it was too dear. He was told, "Sir, you shall pay only forty pistoles. He said, as he drew his last breath, It's too expensive."

His sister, **Marie d'Hautefort** (1616-1691), had a quite extraordinary life. Marie was born in the castle but very soon expressed a wish to see Paris and the royal court. Her wish came true. As lady-in-waiting to Mary of Medici in 1628, she soon came to the notice of **King Louis XIII** and the rest of the court. Her beauty and charms, as much as

her modesty, piety and virtue inspired a veritable passion in the king without **Anne of Austria** feeling offended in any way. After all, the young fair-haired Périgord girl nicknamed **Aurora** because of her beauty might succeed in arousing the royal husband's senses. But Anne was mistaken. Louis and Marie's affair was to remain platonic throughout. **Richelieu** tried to get Marie to spy on the Queen for him but she refused. That meant that she was a declared enemy of the cardinal-duke. Richelieu finally succeeded in separating the King and his favourite by delivering a new mistress to him, **Mlle de la Fayette.** Marie waited patiently until this idyll ended to win back the King's heart. She succeeded but her return to favour was not to last long. Harried by the cardinal, and doubtless tired of Marie's changes of mood and haughty reproaches, Louis XIII sent her into exile. She did not return to Paris until after the death of the cardinal and the King in 1643. She again became the Court's darling at the age of 27, and rejected the most advantageous marriage proposals. As a close friend of the Queen, she did not appreciate the increasing influence of Mazarin. Her continual plottings finally removed her from the Queen's good graces. She was again asked to leave the Court and retired to a convent in 1644. She left it two years later to marry the **Marshal de Schomberg,** Duke of Halluin, at the age of 30. Widowed at 40, she devoted herself to charity work. The woman nicknamed **"the mother of the poor"** by her contemporaries died at the age of 75, considered by many to be a saint.

*Hautefort : rafters
in the south-west tower.*

Périgueux : the R.Isle and Saint-Front Cathedral.

PERIGUEUX

Dordogne's **county town** has relatively little industry, even though it is the largest urban community in the county with a population of 60,000. It does, though, have one unique factory producing postage stamps. Périgueux is very active in the cultural field, providing visitors throughout the year with exhibitions, concerts, drama productions and, recently, with a **Festival of Mime** in the summer.

Gallo-Roman Antiquity meets the Dark Ages : Vesuna and the walled town

Any visit is almost bound to start near the church in the walled town.

Having left your car on the car park, walk down the Rue Romaine to the **Vesuna Tower.** Before you go into the public park, as you stand opposite the tower, you have a good view of the surrounding countryside - the Boissière and Ecornebeuf Hills. This is traditionally said to be the cradle of the town that was the capital of the Petrocorii tribe. The mighty building (it is over 97 ft. high and has an outer diameter of 65 ft.) is, in fact, only the most sacred part of a much larger temple, the area known as the cella. Both sides of the wall are faced with cube-shaped ashlar and the wall is decorated with lines of brick. Below the bricks are gaps that once contained the beams for a peristyle.

As for the outside wall, which can be seen a few yards further on, its longest side ran along some 455 ft., which gives some idea of the size of the building that was probably erected in the 1st century and altered on a number of occasions. Beyond the public park, there is the **Bouquet House.** Amidst the apparent chaos of the dig which has turned up items from various periods (just beside the fence are the remains of an Augustine villa), any enlightened amateur will quickly pick out the 2nd-century construction with the atrium, hypocaust etc.

It appears, though, that with the arrival of the 3rd century and the Lower Empire, Vesuna entered a

decisive phase of its history. The next stage of the walk takes visitors past offices (the main building is the seminary built in the 18th century). They never fail to be surprised at the huge wall at the other end of the railway bridge. For the moment, pass the **Barrière Castle** without stopping and go on to the Roman gate, the so-called **Norman Gate.** At its base is an inextricable mass of bases, columns, capitals and blocks of carved stone and visitors may, just for an instant, believe the legend that persisted for many a long year of a wall built rather hastily during the 3rd century when the hoofbeats of the invader, Alaman, and his troops could be heard approaching. Yet if you go round the wall and look at the other side, you will see that the bonding is as regular as it is strong, which proves that the wall was the result of a project drawn up in high places after long consideration. The wall at the end of the enclosure can be seen at its best when you walk from the Norman Gate to the railway bridge. Here, the variety from one storey to the next and the power of the building itself create a construction that is all the more picturesque because, at the height of the Middle Ages, the Romanesque house (on the left) and the keep of the Barrière Castle were erected over the Roman foundations. The castle belonged to local aristocratic families who held the walled, Christian city from the 5th century onwards, with the Bishop's people. Farm labourers from round about came to seek refuge here whenever invasion threatened. On your way back from the bridge, take a walk through the castle grounds. The building has a whole range of architectural styles from the Classical mediaeval period (13th-century keep) to the Renaissance (16th-century polygonal tower). And remember to give the fine Flamboyant Gothic doorway all the attention that it deserves.

At the height of its splendour, just how important was Vesuna? There is often a tendency to judge it according to the size of the public buildings. The largest is without doubt the one known to local people as the **Arena,** in fact the 1st-century **amphitheatre.** It is a goodly size (it is thought to have been able to take more than 20,000 people) and was based on the design of the Colosseum in Rome.

Périgueux : the Romanesque Vesuna Tower.

Périgueux :
the domes of the cathedral.

The poor condition of the building may come as something of a surprise. As the song says, time has little to do with it. In fact, the amphitheatre was originally an essential part of the 3rd-century wall before being turned into a fortress (Rolphie Castle) by the Counts of Périgord who, during the One Hundred Years' War, became pillagers known for their many acts of villainy. It did not survive the downfall of the wretched noblemen, of whom the most famous of all, Archambaud, joined the English camp. So the fortress was dismantled almost completely on the King's orders at the end of the 14th century.

The visit to the **walled town** ends with the **church.** Anybody wishing to discover all its charms can do no better than read the many descriptions of it written by Jean Secret, the great expert on Périgord's Romanesque architecture. Nobody else has bettered his description of the austere elegance of the domes, the remains of the original building which had four of them until the Wars of Religion. And the two domes, one dating from the late 11th century and the other from the mid 12th century, show how skilfully Périgord incorporated this architectural feature, gradually overcoming the problems of weight. Moreover, by using more and more slender keystones, the region solved the famous problem of squaring a circle - a square at ground level became a dome at the top of the building. The church became a symbol of man's passage from earth to heaven, as well as being a place of salvation.

Périgueux : the market.

Périgueux : the chapter house mill.

LE PUY SAINT FRONT

Take a walk round the outside of the walled town and you will see the **Mataguerre Tower**. It is from the foot of this tower that you begin the visit of the second core around which the town developed - the Puy Saint Front.

The Mataguerre Tower dates from the 14th century and is the only significant remnant of the huge wall that had surrounded the **Puy Saint Front** since the 12th century. In fact, the Puy Saint Front is the name of the village that was built on the slopes of the rise above the R. Isle, said to be the site of the tomb of the apostle of Périgord. It was probably the expansion in trade in the 11th century and the increased popularity of pilgrimages (Le Puy-Saint-Front was an important stage on the road to Compostella) that caused this village to become such a bustling community. The population of the commercially-minded village, the burghers of Saint-Front, were soon embroiled in quarrels with the lay or ecclesiastical aristocracy of the walled town whose authority they accepted with great difficulty. At the end of the 13th century, Louis IX united the rival communities, thereby putting an end to the disputes that often flared up on the Place Francheville (the so-called Entre-deux-villes, or Between-two-towns). Until the 14th century, the village underwent a remarkable period of expansion. Just take a look at the narrow streets that lead up to the cathedral, e.g. the Rue des Farges, and you can imagine what everyday life was like in such a densely-populated town. There were no less than 2,400 homes and more than 10,000 people in an area equivalent to less than one-sixth of the present town.

From the **Place Hoche**, continue your walk through the Middle Ages along the **Rue du Calvaire**. In it, behind a studded gate, is the 12th-century **Viguier Residence**, now Saint Front School. The street leads to the **Place de la Clautre** where visitors see the most controversial building in the entire region - **Saint Front Cathedral**. Or is it cathedrals ? Part of the building that can be seen from the end of the Rue du Calvaire is doubly unusual. It is the oldest section, built in the late 10th century when Frotaire was Bishop of Périgueux, and its West Front includes features dating from Antiquity and the Merovingian period and re-used here. The building devoid of a roof standing in front of the belltower to which it should be connected, is an open courtyard which was obviously intended to have a dome. The 12th-century belltower, almost 200 ft. high, is also exactly as it was when it was first built. The same cannot be said of the second church, the cathedral itself. It stands in the shape of a Cross, as it was after the 19th-century rebuilding project.

Inside the building, its coldness tends to be forgotten because of the purity of the double domes. Visitors are also moved by the beautiful reredos made to the glory of the Virgin Mary, depicting the Assumption. You may also like to ask to see the cloisters. During the peak tourist season, there is a **guided tour.**

On leaving the cathedral, head for the river. On the left is the **Chapter's Mill** which has recently been restored. It shows the site of the former mill-race which started at the Tournepiche Bridge, now the Barris Bridge. Across the bridge are two fine mansions which, taken together, constitute what the people of Périgueux traditionally call the **Consuls' House** despite the fact that it has nothing to do with local government.

The **Cayla Mansion** is reminiscent of the residences in the Rue Aubergerie. It has the same archaic mediaeval structures but has blended them with Flamboyant Gothic in the decoration of the dormer windows. On the left, the rather feverish grace of the colonettes on the **Lambert Mansion** takes us back to the days of François I and the Italian Campaign.

Cross the road and, a few yards further on, take the **Rue du Port de Graule.** Stop at the entrance to the street, a reminder of the old working-class Périgueux, and look down to the other end. It is easy to see why it was chosen as a background for films set in the recent or

more distant past, such as Stellio Lorenzi's *Jacquou.* The street has a damp, insalubrious appearance yet it is a veritable treasure trove of carvings and sculptures.

At the end of the Rue du Port de Graule, there is a very interesting succession of alleyways. Go up the flight of steps to the **Avenue Daumesnil** then turn straight into the **Rue du Plantier** on your left. Go down the **Rue Notre Dame,** the **Rue des Francs-Maçons,** the **Rue de la Constitution** and finally the **Rue de la Nation.** Yet it is almost certainly in the central part of Le Puy-Saint-Front, the area around the **Rue Limogeanne,** that the finest restora-

Périgueux : the ruins of the Barrière Castle.

tion work has been carried out over the past ten years with the aim of giving the town back all its own particular attractiveness. If you want to make the best of the charms scattered throughout this district during the Renaissance, take the **Rue de la Clarté** and you will see, on the right, an 18th-century house, the birthplace of the man who has gone down in history because of his famous answer to a call for surrender ("I will surrender Vincennes when you surrender my leg" - he had lost it in a previous battle) - General Daumesnil. From there, take the **Rue Salinière** and the **Rue du Serment** which leads to the **Place de l'Hôtel de Ville.** It was here that Voltaire's rival, Lagrange Chancel, lived. His epigrams aimed at the Crown Prince were famous in the Age of Enlightenment. At no. 7, there is a 15th-century house with a graceful polygonal staircase tower. From there, you enter the main shopping street, with the hustle and bustle of the **Rue Limogeanne.** It has a succession of fine mansions, but the most outstanding is the **Estignard Residence.** The best way of reaching it is to take the alleyway immediately to the right. It leads to two charming, almost Italianate squares which in turn lead to the **Rue de la Miséricorde.** This is an excellent place from which to admire the **Estignard Residence.** Note the mullioned dormer windows flanked by stone greyhounds.

Let's finish our stroll with two museums. The **Périgord Museum** on the edge of the Tourny promenade houses some remarkable prehistoric collections and a large section on Périgord's Gallo-Roman antiquities. In the Rue des Farges is the **Military Museum.**

Périgueux : the cloisters next to Saint-Front Cathedral.

102

Jumilhac : the castle.

JUMILHAC LE GRAND
31 miles E. of Nontron

On the northernmost border of Green Périgord, on the edge of the Limousin Region, in an area of fertile valleys, **Jumilhac Castle** looks down from its clifftop at the waters of the R. Isle, which here is little more than a swift-flowing stream at the bottom of a gorge. In 1579, a rich farmer and blacksmith, **Antoine Chapelle,** married the heiress to the estate. Antoine Chapelle had amas-

Jumilhac : West Front and roofs.
In the centre is the "Marquis' hat".

sed his fortune through trading in iron and was able to finance the campaigns of the future Henri IV. In gratitude, the King visited Jumilhac Castle and knighted him in 1597.

The new nobleman then had the 13th- and 14th-century fortress replaced by the present castle, built in a Gothic style that was a bit old-fashioned at a time when people preferred airier constructions. The castle, which is **open to the public,** looks like something out of a fairy-tale, bristling with towers and roofs. Built of reddish brown cristalline schist, it seems to have been constructed to no particular plan, rather more for decoration than for living in. The main building, lit by Renaissance windows, has corbelled turrets. The **roofs,** described by Gustave Doré as the most **romantic** anywhere in France, lift their pepperpots and chimneys high above the "Marquis' hat" at the top of a tall turret. The leaden finials above the ridge tile represent birds, angels, various characters and crockets.

A room near the entrance retraces Jumilhac's history. On the second floor, is a small room with semi-circular arching and walls decorated with naive frescoes containing a bed and a spinning wheel. The door is decorated with a **portrait** known as **"The Spinner",** painted by an anonymous artist. It is a picture of Louise d'Hautefort, who was locked away for twenty years by her husband, Antoine Chapelle's son, Antoine II de Jumilhac.

Saint-Jean-de-Côle : La Marthonie Castle.

ST. JEAN DE COLE
12 miles N.E. of Brantôme

St. Jean de Côle is a charming little **village** through which flows the R. Côle, a cool stream full of waterfalls crossed by an old humpbacked **Gothic bridge** with pierheads. The Périgord-style houses roofed with brown tiles earned the village the title of "the finest roofs in France". The main square is closed off on the right-hand side by **La Marthonie Castle** and, at the end, by a huge **church** and the **priory** behind a **covered market** with some quite extraordinary rafters. The church and Augustinian priory were built between 1086 and 1099 by the Bishop of Périgueux, Renaud de Thiviers, just before he set out for the Holy Land.

The fine grey granite **church** with the tile roof is built to a layout that is unique in Périgord. The huge, tall, square nave, with only one span, is topped by a dome measuring 41 ft. in diameter (the biggest in the region). The flattened section of the dome collapsed on several occasions over the centuries and has now been replaced by a floor. At the end of the nave is a pentagonal apse and two

Saint-Jean-de-Côle : rafters in the covered market.

Saint-Jean-de-Côle : the Romanesque church and covered market.▶

radiating chapels of the same size. The interior is a blend of austere **Romanesque architecture** and 17th-century decoration. Outside, in addition to the massive two-storey rectangular belltower dating from the 17th century, note the chevet and the chapel decorated with supporting arches on column-piers with **carved capitals** illustrating Biblical scenes - Daniel in the lions' den, God shaping Adam's face, angels, Noah's drunkenness, and the Annunciation. Beneath the roof of the three chapels are some 75 modillions with carvings of masks, monsters, wrestlers, obscene characters and various animals.

In addition to the church, the **priory** in St. Jean de Côle still has its 17th-century sacristy, residences dating from the 17th and 18th centuries, and a **library** with a ceiling painted by Lesueur. A medallion shows an "ecstasy of St. Paul" attributed to Lebrun. There is also the prior's lodgings, two sides of two-storey Renaissance cloisters, and the abbey millwheel originally turned by the waters of the R. Côle.

Next to the abbey is **La Marthonie Castle** which is **open to the public.** It dates from the 15th and 16th centuries.

Villars : the ruins of Boschaud Abbey.

VILLARS
8 miles N.E. of Brantôme

Villars, whose Périgord-style houses nestle round its Romanesque church, could very well be nicknamed , "the village of three marvels".

Half-a mile to the north, the architecture of the very elegant **Puyguil-** hem **Castle** is reminiscent of the harmony of Loire Valley castles. This "Azay le Rideau" of Périgord, the best-preserved of all the Renaissance castles in the south-west of France,

was born in 1466. He was President of the Bordeaux Assizes and, later, of the courts in Paris and was entrusted by François I with the administration of the kingdom after the sovereign's departure for Italy. He died in Blois in 1517.

Preceded by a tree-lined avenue, Puyguilhem lies in a rustic setting. It has a large central building flanked on the right by a large **round tower** with an adjacent octagonal staircase tower and on the left by a pentagonal tower with a pyramid-shaped roof. At the back of the building are two wings of unequal length. The north wing beyond the round tower dates from the Renaissance period, while the one on the south side is 18th century. The front of the central building is decorated with mullioned windows and a traceried balustrade beneath three very fine dormer windows and an elegant roof with a magnificent carved chimney. Note the moulded frieze on the parapet walk and, at the bottom of the uppermost dormer window, a bust of a man and two of women in a medallion. Higher up, the finely-carved pyramid-shaped gable is topped by the statue of a person standing up. The staircase tower, like the tower in front, is decorated in the Louis XII style. Beneath the windows are large panels carved with letters in a plethora of pearls, cords, chains, and crowns. Beneath the roof, a stringcourse bears a whole series of letters, seemingly put together to form a secret code. At the other end of the façade is the main staircase, inside a five-sided tower dating from the reign of François I. The **capitals** on the door are carved with human faces and the lintel shows a chalice held by two cherubs. The visit of the interior begins with the guardroom and the round tower with its slit windows and fireplace carved with medallions. The kitchen still has its original utensils and a large table. Beyond the dining room is a large chamber with a fine decorated fireplace. Among the **furniture** is a carved Flemish oak chest, a Spanish coffer, and an Aubusson tapestry. Visitors then mount a beautiful **grand staircase** with a splendid coffered ceiling that has hanging key-

is **open to the public.** The present castle was built in the 16th century, probably by **Mandot de la Marthonie,** and was completed by his two brothers, Jean and Gaston, successive Bishops of Dax from 1514 to 1555. The old La Marthonie family owned the neighbouring estate of St. Jean de Côle as far back as 1313. Its most illustrious member, Mandot,

Villars : the Château de Puiguilhem.

second floor, visitors are shown the admirable chestnut rafters in the shape of an upturned boat. The visit ends at the pentagonal tower from which there is a view of the pediments above the dormer windows on the façade. From the terrace, there is a vast panoramic view of the surrounding countryside.

Half-a-mile to the west is **Boschaud Abbey,** founded in 1154, one of the four **Cistercian** abbeys in Périgord with Peyrouze, Cadouin and le Dalon. It is **open to the public** and is a unique example of a Cistercian abbey with a church bearing a line of **domes.** Now in ruins, the church had a three-span nave topped by three or four slender domes. All that remains today is the chancel and part of the transept whose dome has been rebuilt. Flanked by two semi-circular apsidal chapels, the barrel-vaulted apse has three bays, one of them decorated with colonettes. Boschaud still has some of the abbey buildings (the chapter house with ogival windows, a Romanesque sacristy, the remains of the cloisters, a dorter, and apartments) and some of the outer wall is still standing. Although very badly damaged by the passage of time, Boschaud has been the object of a major restoration project since 1971 led by the Old Manor Club.

Three miles to the N.E., the **Villars Cave** (or Cluzeau Cave, "cluzeau" meaning "lookout post") with its many stalactites and stalagmites is **open to the public.** In addition to the outstanding **rock formations,** it has some thirty **paintings** and engravings 15,000 to 17,000 years old. The long entrance tunnel is marked with yellow, red and black dots. Among the most interesting figures is the famous **"blue horse"** and, at the end of the cave as in Lascaux, the drawing of a man being attacked by a bison. During the visit of the section laid out for visitors, there is a veritable underground fairytale land - stoops, rock falls, eccentrics, cascades, candles, ceilings of stalactites, drapes, all stretching over several hundred yards. The cave also has noticeable traces of occupation by bears.

stones and bases carved with letters. The ribs are supported on carvings of animals (bulls, lion etc.) and plants. On the first floor, one of the chambers houses one of the rarest items on show - a huge fireplace with a mantel divided into niches. It is decorated with sculptures representing six of the twelve labours of Hercules, a veritable masterpiece. On the

Brantôme : the R. Dronne, abbey and church.

BRANTOME
17 miles N. of Périgueux

Wrapped in a meander of the R. Dronne, the small town of Brantôme (pop. 2,000) was nicknamed the "Venice of Périgord" by President Raymond Poincarré when he visited it in 1913. It is an island floating on the green waters of the river, a jewel set in the ripples of the stream, gathering its mediaeval and Renaissance houses up tight and lit by the white mass of its **abbey.**

At the beginning of the Christian era, a community is said to have lived in the **underground shelters** at La Fontaine du Rocher, and St.

Front is said to have destroyed a statue of Mercury there. As for the Benedictine abbey of which the town was so proud, it is thought to have been founded c. 769 or 786 A.D. Charlemagne is said to have given the brand new monastery the relics of St. Sicaire, a victim of the Massacre of the Holy Innocents. Ransacked by the Vikings a few years later, it was rebuilt at the end of the 10th century. Thereafter, town and abbey underwent joint expansion. Du Guesclin came to chase the English out of the town and learnt that he had been made Constable of France. From 1538 onwards, the Abbot of Brantôme, Pierre de Mareuil, had a right-angled bridge built over the

river, an elegant Renaissance pavilion and a number of resting places in the Monks' Garden. He was succeeded by his nephew, **Pierre de Bourdeille,** better-known as Brantôme (for his biography, see Bourdeilles). He was given charge of the abbey in 1557. On his death in 1614, Brantôme Abbey was the most prosperous community in Aquitaine. But it quickly fell into decline. During the Revolution, its rich collection of books and the last seven monks were dispersed.

On the banks of the R. Dronne, on the Boulevard Charlemagne, stands the massive white abbey and its church, **St. Peter's.** In this Romanes-

113

*Brantôme : the Medici Fountain
and bronze statue of Pierre de Bourdeille.*

◀*Brantôme : arguably the oldest belltower in France.*

que and Gothic edifice, the two-span nave topped by 12th-century domes was thought to have had ribbed arching of the Anjou type during the Gothic Era. Nowadays, visitors see a building that underwent complete restoration in the middle of last century, under the leadership of the architect Abadie. In the chancel with its flat chevet lit by three bays are two carved wooden panels, one opposite the other. They were the work of a 17th-century monk. The one on the left illustrates Emperor Charlemagne handing St. Sicaire's relics over to the Abbot of Brantôme. The bas-relief on the right shows the Massacre of the Holy Innocents, a theme that is taken up again in a 19th-century sculpture to the right of the nave and on a 12th- or 13th-century bas-relief in the porch. There is one Romanesque capital remaining, now used as a stoop, and a very fine 14th-century carving of Christ's Baptism.

On the north side of the church, standing 195 ft. high, the Brantôme **belltower** is undoubtedly the most beautiful of its kind anywhere in Périgord. Recent investigations date its construction in the Carolingian and even Visigoth period, which would make it the **oldest belltower in France.** It consists of four storeys, each set slightly back from each other (plus a room underground), and the top is decorated with **gables.** It has a pyramid-shaped stone roof

115

*Brantôme : the Renaissance pavilion
and the right-angled bridge over the R. Dronne.*

classical staircase devoid of pillars leads to two large chambers. In the former monks' dorter, there are some wonderful rafters in the shape of an upturned boat. Various exhibitions are held there. Inside the abbey, a three-section museum has a variety of prehistoric collections, some furniture and paintings, as well as that the very strange mediumistic works of the engraver and painter Fernand Desmoulin (1857-1914). Hidden away behind the abbey are St. Sicaire's fountain said to help with fertility problems and refurbished caves, reminders of troglodyte houses. One of them bears carvings by an unknown craftsman, "Triumph of Death" or "The Last Judgement" (late 15th century) and "The Crucifixion" (16th or 17th century). The cave has been made into a theatre.

A few yards away opposite St. Roch's Tower, is an elegant **Renaissance pavilion** (now the Tourist Office) with mullioned windows flanked by pilasters and colonettes. Its door bears the coat-of-arms of Pierre de Mareuil. It stands guard over the small **right-angled bridge** with pierheads that crosses the R. Dronne. There is a superb view of the abbey, the waterwheel and the river's vegetation from here. The bridge leads to the park, originally the "Monks' Garden" where strollers can take a breather on the benches of the great **resting-places** dating from the 16th century.

Brantôme is not only the tourist capital of North Périgord, it is also the setting for intense cultural activity culminating in summer with the International Festival of Classical Ballet which was founded in 1958 by Jacqueline Rayet. The Last Judgement Grotto provides a magical backdrop for the festival, bringing dancers and 1,200 spectators together for an age-old rite - the worship of beauty.

*The « Pierre Levée »
(Standing Stone)
east of Brantôme.*

and, on each of its storeys pierced with bay windows, there are archaic capitals carved with foliage and interlacing.

All that remains of the Renaissance cloisters is one gallery, and a small chapter house with Flamboyant Gothic vaulting and ribbed columns. The gallery leads into the Benedictine abbey that now belongs to the town. The 17th-century buildings are **open to the public.** A fine

BOURDEILLES
15 miles N.W. of Périgueux

In its picturesque setting high above the R. Dronne and overlooking the village, Bourdeilles is in fact two castles in one - a **mediaeval fortress** and a **Renaissance residence.** Historically, the first trace of a Lord of Bourdeille goes back to 1044. At that time, he was an important person, one of Périgord's four barons.

The estate then became the subject of numerous family disputes and the barons paid homage in turn to the Abbots of Brantôme, the King of France, the King of England, and the Count of Périgord. In 1259, St. Louis gave the castle to the English. A few years later, **Géraut de Maumont,** Councillor to Philip the Fair, took it by storm and, from 1283 to 1298, had the fortress built. The Renaissance castle was commissio-

ned by **Jacquette de Montbron,** widow of the Périgord Seneschal André de Bourdeille and Brantôme's sister-in-law. She drew the plans herself for a house that was designed to accommodate Catherine of Medici, as required by tradition, although the Queen never, in fact, came here. The lady of the manor died in 1598 before the work was completed and without seeing the wonderful ceilings that the Italian painter from the Fon-

Bourdeilles : the mediaeval fortress and Renaissance château.

tainebleau school, **Ambroise Le Noble,** decorated during his stay in Bourdeilles from 1641 to 1644.

Before visiting the castle, let us just mention a person whose name is forever linked to Bourdeilles - **Pierre de Bourdeille,** known as "Brantôme" (1538-1614). He was the third son in the family and was therefore destined for an ecclesiastical career. In 1557, Henri II granted him the income of Brantôme Abbey.

But he had little taste for the life of a cleric and was never ordained a priest. He travelled a great deal, firstly in Italy in 1558 and 1559. Then he accompanied the unfortunate Queen of France, Mary Stuart, to her Scottish exile in 1561. A short stay at the Court of Charles IX and there he was, waging war with François de Guise against the Protestants, before setting off again on his travels. In 1564, he joined the Spanish

army and fought in Morocco then travelled on to Portugal. In 1566, the abbot was to be found in Malta, participating in the crusade against the Turks. At this point, he may even have been a sort of pirate. He took part in warfare all over France until 1569, when illness forced him to stay in his abbey for almost one year. In true conquistador-style, he prepared an expedition to Peru but the project did not get off the ground. In 1582,

after the death of his elder brother, he lost his inheritance and Henri III refused to grant him the title of Seneschal of Périgord. He then considered betraying his country to Spain but a serious riding accident crippled him for life. Broken physically but not morally, he lived from 1583 to 1587 in Brantôme Abbey or in Richemont Castle which he had had built. He spent all his time writing. After a brief stay at the Court, he retired to his estate for the last time. He died on 5th July 1614 in Richemont Castle. His works were published posthumously in Leyde, in Holland. Nowadays, his two best-known works are *Lives of Foreign Illustrious Men and Great Leaders* and his masterpiece, *Lives of Gallant Ladies,* a biting portrait gallery and collection of lively, spicy tales. Brantôme may not have been a great prose-writer, but his Gascon verve and his memories of an adventurous life, his prowesses and his boastfulness are all highly attractive.

Bourdeilles Castle, which has belonged to the County Council since 1960, is **open to the public.** From the entrance flanked by two 15th-century round machicolated towers, you can see the Renaissance arcade at the Seneschal's entrance and the doorway to the private chapel on the right. The gateway leads to the courtyard where the two castles stand. The fortress built by Géraud de Maumont, Councillor to Philip the Fair at the end of the 13th century, underwent modifications in the 16th century. On the site of the former mediaeval residence, there is a courtyard paved with smooth pebbles which contains a well. It is surrounded on all sides by high walls. They have bay windows with ledges and are topped by parapet walks dominated by the impressive **octagonal keep** 124 ft. high, built in the early 14th century and justifiably considered as being the finest in Périgord. It contains dungeons and three storeys with ribbed vaulting lit by slit-windows. The spiral staircase leads up to the crenelations at the top

Bourdeilles :
the 14th century octagonal keep.

from which there is a view over the whole of Bourdeilles. The buildings adjacent to the tower include a huge chamber with semi-circular vaulting on the first floor, paved with pebbles and lit by a twin 13th-century window. The rectangular Renaissance castle has been turned into a **museum** housing a very interesting collection of 16th- and 17th-century furniture, most of it from Burgundy and Spain. There are also numerous suits of armour and works of art, among them a reproduction of the Bayeux Tapestry, and a magnificent "Descent into the Tomb" with eight characters on it dating from the 16th century, a 13th-century wooden statue of Christ. On the first floor in the dining room with the Renaissance fireplace, the walls are adorned with 16th- and 17th-century tapestries and portraits. Bourdeilles' main attraction, though, is the gilded drawing room 49 ft. by 33 ft. with monumental fireplaces and a ceiling and panelling decorated by Ambroise Le Noble. The room contains a fine collection of furniture and some fine 16th- and 17th-century tapestries.

BERGERAC

Bergerac, the sub-prefecture of the County of Dordogne, is the second-largest town in the county with a population of 30,000. It is also the capital of south-west Périgord, lying in a region that is open to the Bordeaux area and that might be called the "Wine Country". Bergerac is a busy industrial centre in a region that is otherwise mainly concerned with agriculture and wine-growing. One of its industries is the Poudrerie Nationale, one of the largest companies in Périgord. There is also the large National Tobacco Institute Research Centre, because Dordogne is a major producer. Finally, it has a major intellectual role. But here it is first and foremost **vineyards** that dominate the countryside as much as the local economy. The 40,000 hectares of vineyard produce 75 % of the county's total production. All the winegrowers' associations offer some of their precious beverage for tasting, especially the ones in Bergerac

Bourdeilles : the Renaissance palace that once belonged to Jacquette de Montbron. Beyond it is the top of the fortress keep.

and Monbazillac which are open to the public. From the north-east to the north-west of the region, Bergerac's wines are Pécharmant, a connoisseurs favourite, the fruity Rosette, the red or white Côtes de Bergerac, and the sweet white Montravel so beloved of Montaigne. In the south is Monbazillac, the most famous of all the region's wines and, near Sigoulès, the Saussignac that won Rabelais' praises.

Although the town was the birth-place of a few figures who have con-tributed to the glory of France, like the philosopher Maine de Biran, it has to be said that the most famous of all Bergerac's sons never experienced "the green sweetness of evenings on the Dordogne". The philosopher, essayist and dramatist, **Savinien de Cyrano** (born in Paris in 1619, died in Sannois (Val d'Oise) in 1655), author of *The Death of Agrippine, A Voyage to the Moon* (1657) and *With some Account of the Solar World* (1662), was a true Parisian. When he entered the Company of

Guards of Gascony, he quite naturally took the name Bergerac because he did, indeed, own the "Bergerac" (now the Sous Forêts) estate near Dampierre in Yvelines (Seine-et-Oise).

This insanely brave writer, whose thinking was as free as his morals, this passionate science enthusiast and forerunner of the Age of Enlightenment "is nothing but a Parisian Gascon", one might say!

And it was indeed Edmond Rostand who, in 1897, in his still-famous play, made Cyrano a Gascon full of wit with a legendary nose, a man who was as skilful a warrior as he was a poet. He used, in his play, people who really had existed in the life of the real Cyrano and his strange death also appears to be totally

authentic. Yet legend dies hard, and denying its tales would still make more than one Périgord man shiver. So let's make the best of a bad job. Although Cyrano was not really from Périgord, at least he made Bergerac famous throughout France.

Bergerac's history since the Middle Ages can be summed up in three words - the river, the wine, and the bridge. Although the R. Dordogne was the route taken by barbarian, Arab and Viking invaders, it was also and more importantly the reason for the region's economic expansion. Bergerac became a major port for lighters travelling up- and down-river between Auvergne and the Bordeaux region. Towards the 11th century, when Bergerac lay on the road to Compostella, it was given a bridge

around which the town gradually began to develop. From that time onwards, Bergerac's wines started to refresh dry English and Dutch throats. In 1254, quarrels broke out concerning the heirs to the Rudel estate. The family owned the town and the disputes gave the English an opportunity to gain a foothold in western Périgord. It took intervention by Du Guesclin to liberate the town. In the 12th century, Bergerac was declared a free town, i.e. a community that was not under the authority of a lord, but consular power was not really set up until one century later. In 1546, the Calvinist faith became deeply rooted among the intelligentsia and upper middle classes, thanks to the influence of the Queen of Navarre and her Court

Bergerac.

who had settled in the neighbouring town of Nérac.

Bergerac extended the warmest of welcomes to Jeanne d'Albret and her son, Henri of Navarre, in 1568. After the St. Bartholomew's Day Massacre in 1572, it became, as Pierre Barrière put it, "the intellectual capital of the Protestant world". But in 1620, the town was invaded by royal troops. Richelieu had the ramparts razed to the ground in 1629. Many Huguenots then emigrated to Holland and England.

The old town is bounded by the river and the Rue St. Esprit, Rue Neuve, Rue d'Arganson and Rue de la Résistance. All these streets were laid along the line of the former ramparts. Near the former convent of the Ladies of Faith, now the town hall, the **Peyrarède Residence,** or Henri IV's Castle, houses the only **Tobacco Museum** in France, which retraces the history of "Nicot's weed" that was imported in the 16th century. In 1674, its cultivation was regulated in France. The monopoly created in 1816 limited its production to the Agen region, Périgord and Quercy. The harvests provided the farmers with a stable income despite the threat of replacing dark tobacco by light. The museum has four sections : a history of tobacco, a presentation of the techniques used (growing, manufacture, marketing), a collection of smokers' objects, and a collection of works of art (paintings, pottery) on the common theme of tobacco. The Peyrarède Residence also houses a local history museum with an interesting section on prehistory.

The former **Recollect Convent** still has two wings of its cloisters. The building, which is open to the public, is a blend of 14th and 17th-century architectural elements. It is the headquarters of the Interprofessional Bergerac Wine Council and is used for receptions and enthronements of the Vintage.

The **Rue de la Myrpe,** one of the most attractive streets in the town, is adorned with timbered houses, some of them made of wattle and daub. The Rue des Conférences owes its names to the Peace Treaty of Bergerac (1577) signed by the King of Navarre and the representatives of Henri III, thereby putting an end to the 6th War of Religion. In it is a

Museum of Wine and River Traffic. After admiring the fountain of the Place Pelissière, visitors arrive at St. James' Church, which was already mentioned in the 11th century and used as a stopping place on the road to Compostella. It was destroyed during the Wars of Religion and restored in the 19th century, but it still has its belltower and Flamboyant Gothic windows. Nearby is a Museum of Sacred Art.

The Rue Saint James, with its 15th- and 16th-century houses, and the Rue des Fontaines with its 14th-century "Old Inn" are two of the most picturesque thoroughfares and a pleasant place for a stroll. The "Charles IX House" on the Place du Marché was visited by the said king on 8th August 1565.

The Château de Monbazillac and its vineyards.

MONBAZILLAC
4 miles S. of Bergerac

Standing in the midst of a vineyard just beside the village, **Monbazillac Castle** which is **open to the public,** was built c. 1550 by François d'Aydié and his wife, Françoise de Salignac. It was completed by Charles d'Aydié and Jeanne de Bourdeille and passed through the Wars of Religion and the Peasants' Revolt unscathed. It has remained almost untouched since the Renaissance and is therefore highly authentic. The main building flanked by four great round towers has a façade with mullioned windows. A crenelated parapet walk topped by tall dormer windows runs round the castle. The roof of russet tiles above the grey stone building has fleur-de-lys weathervanes. A dry moat completes the defensive system of this secular castle which, although built in the 16th century, has a decidedly mediaeval appearance.

The castle belongs to the Monbazillac Winegrowers Association and houses a number of **museums.** The reception hall with French-style ceiling has a monumental 16th-century fireplace and two 17th-century Flemish tapestries. As you wander through the rooms, you will see Périgord furniture, engravings and old

maps, medals, drawings by Sem, a Périgord-born caricaturist who worked at the turn of the century, and a history of the Protestant faith in the Bergerac region, for the castle was used for many years as a Protestant church. On the first floor is a reconstitution of Viscountess of Monbazillac's Louis XIII-style bedchamber. The cellars, of course, house a Wine Museum (with wine-tasting room and the possibility of buying direct from the castle). There is a 4-hectare park and, from the terrace, an extensive panoramic view of the vineyards, the valley and Bergerac.

Anybody interested in good wine will recognise Monbazillac Castle on the labels of the region's most famous wine. The vineyard that produces this wonderfully-fruity sweet white wine, covers some 3,000 hectares. Created by monks in the 11th century, it underwent rapid expansion in the 17th century when exports to Holland increased dramatically.

SAINT-MICHEL-DE-MONTAIGNE
25 miles W. of Bergerac

On the borders of the counties of Gironde and Dordogne, in a **castle**

open to the public set in the midst of vineyards that produce a sweet white wine called Montravel appreciated by the philosopher himself, we find the most famous of all Périgord's sons, one of the thinkers who was a guiding light for humanity, **Michel de Montaigne** (1533-1592). On his father's side, he came from a family of newly-titled merchants and, on his mother's side, he was descended from rich Spanish Jews. Montaigne was born in the castle on 28th February 1533. In 1554 at the age of 21, when his father was Mayor of Bordeaux, he was named Councillor at the Customs and Excise Dept. in Périgueux. He entered Bordeaux Assizes in 1557 and became friendly with the young man from Sarlat, **Etienne de La Boétie,** who was three years older than him. Their exemplary friendship lasted for 6 years, until the man Montaigne considered as his mentor in philosophy died on 18th August 1563. He married Françoise de la Chassaigne on 22nd September 1565 and had six daughters. Only one of them survived. When his father died in 1568, he became Lord of Montaigne and claimed his Périgord background for all to hear. He parodied Caesar and had no hesitation in writing "and I would like myself better being second or third in adventure in Périgueux than first in Paris". After selling his charge as Councillor at the Assizes, he retired to his estate in 1571. In 1572, the year of the St. Bartholomew's Day Massacre, he started to write his *Essays*. Until 1580, he seldom left his castle and, although Henri of Navarre named him Gentleman of the Bedchamber, he devoted all his time to writing the first two sections of his work. On 1st March 1580, the first edition of the Essays was published. Montaigne went to Paris to present his book to Henri III then undertook a long trip through France, Switzerland and Italy. On 7th September 1581, in Lucques, he learnt that he had been made Mayor of Bordeaux for two years. By 30th November, he was back in Montaigne. During his last two mandates; while continuing to correct his Essays, Montaigne made a name for himself by his tolerance and his desire to preserve peace. In December 1584, he welcomed the future King Henri IV to his castle. In 1585, the Black Death forced him to leave the town. He retired to his castle where he devoted himself wholeheartedly to his writing, a rest period that was only interrupted by the arrival of Henri of Navarre in 1587 shortly after the Battle of Coutras. Still working on changes to his Essays to which he devoted twenty years of his life, Montaigne died in his castle on 13th September 1592.

Montaigne's **castle,** which suffered serious fire damage in the 19th century, was rebuilt in a Neo-Renaissance style which has a certain striking quality about it. After crossing a gateway and entering a courtyard surrounded by high walls, visitors come to the only part of the 16th-century castle to have survived, and the object of numerous literary pilgrimages - the round "library" tower joined onto a tall square building by a staircase tower. On the ground floor is the chapel and a small room from which Montaigne followed the services. A spiral staircase and low door lead to the storey with the "room devoid of all that is unnecessary", the library, a spartan room heated by a plain fireplace. The **beams** and joists in the ceiling bear some 54 painted or engraved Greek, Latin, Stoic, Epicurian and sceptical **mottos,** a veritable synthesis of Montaigne's philosophy. The landscape that can be seen from the windows still holds memories of the thinker - the path where he used to stroll, the curtain walls where he had intended to have a quiet parapet walk built for his exercise. The castle terrace provides a fine panoramic view of the Lidoire Valley.

Saint-Michel-de-Montaigne : it was in this tranquil solitude that Michel de Montaigne wrote his ''Essays''. The photograph shows the château roof, rebuilt after a fire..

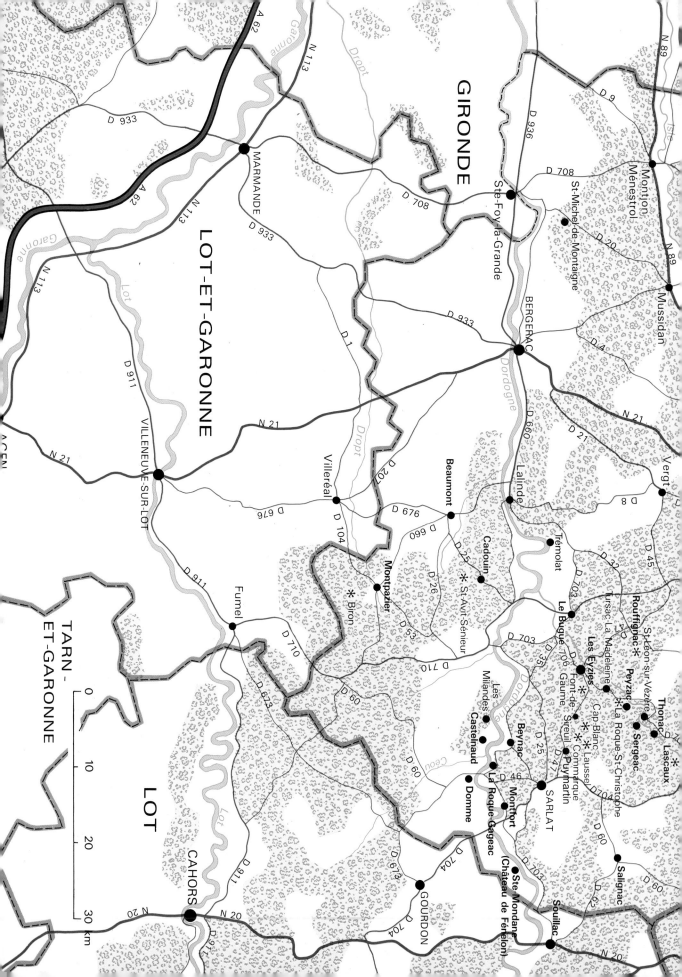

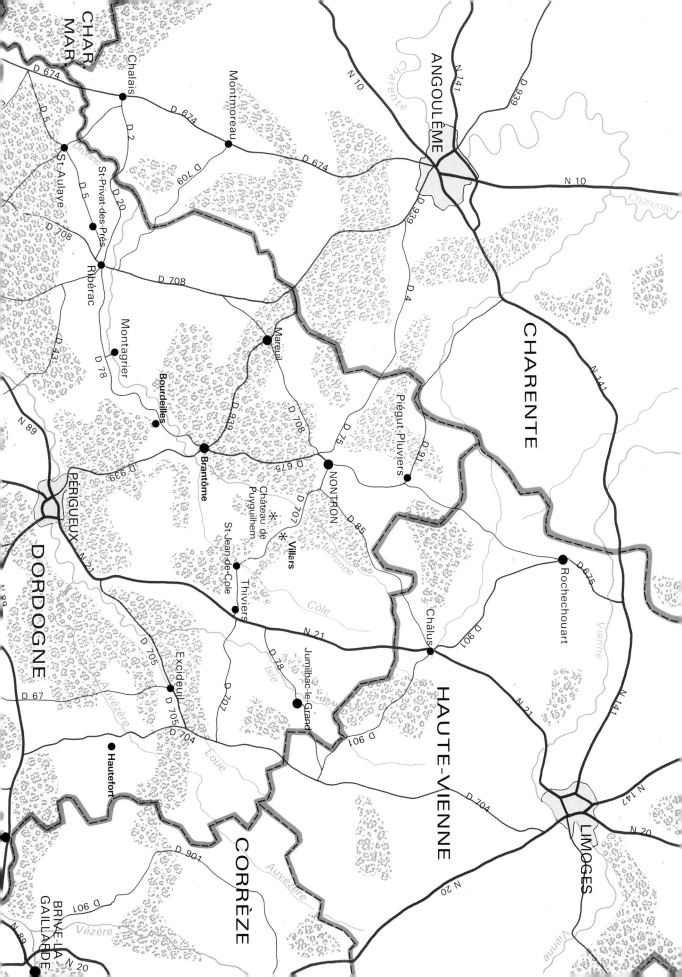

TABLE OF CONTENTS

The photos of Perigueux are by Hervé Boulé, and those of the paintings of the prehistoric sites are by Hervé Champollion.
by Patrick Mérienne

Cet ouvrage a été imprimé par Aubin Imprimeur à Ligugé (86).
I.S.B.N. 2.7373.0070.7 - Dépôt légal : janvier 1988
N° éditeur : 1408.02.09.01.91